ISBN-13:
978-1725043527

ISBN-10:
1725043521

DRAG411's Ten Black Books

Book 1:	**DRAG411's "DRAG Bully, A Survivor's Guide"**
	Copyright © 2015 and 2018
Book 2:	**DRAG411's "Original DRAG Handbook"**
	Copyright © 2010, 2011, 2012, 2014, and 2018
Book 3:	**DRAG411's "Crown Me! Winning Pageants"**
	Copyright © 2013, 2014, and 2018
Book 4:	**DRAG411's "DRAG King Guide"**
	Copyright © 2014 and 2018
Book 5:	**DRAG411's "DRAG Stories"**
	Copyright © 2011, 2014, and 2018
Book 6:	**DRAG411's "DRAG Mother, DRAG Father"**
	Copyright © 2012, 2014, and 2018
Book 7:	**DRAG411's "Spotlight Today"**
	Copyright © 2012 and 2018
Book 8:	**DRAG411's "DRAG Queen Guide"**
	Copyright © 2014 and 2018
Book 9:	Two Comedy Scripts:
	DRAG411's "Best Said Dead"
	Copyright © 2011, 2014, and 2018
	"Following Wynter"
	Copyright © 2012, 2014, and 2018
Book 10:	**DRAG411's "DRAG World"**
	Copyright © 2012 and 2018

From the best-selling author of "CommUnity of Transition,"
"Two Days Past Dead," The Novel and the sequel,
"Turn Around Bright Eyes, The DRAG Queen Killer,"
"Joey Brooks, The Show Must Go On,"
And "Waiting On God."

DRAG411's

DRAG Bully
A Survivor's Guide

2nd Edition

I am not a fan of the term "drag" as applied across this entire art form, but until they find a single word "more accepting," I will have to use it. The drag community has helped me earn twenty LGBT world records. I created DRAG411 to document this form of entertainment. We are the world's largest organization for male, female, and androgynous impersonators with over 7,000 current or former impersonators in 32 countries.   The Infamous Todd Kachinski Kottmeier

(sic)

Latin adverb: thus"; in full: sic erat scriptum, thus was it written indicates DRAG411 transcribed the comments into this book exactly as found in the original source, complete with any erroneous or archaic spelling or other nonstandard presentation. We try to print the responses using the same words sent to us, ensuring the reader DRAG411 did not change the tone, reflection, or character of each response.

We print verbatim, without editing

ver·ba·tim   vər'bātəm/
adverb: verbatim; adjective
in exactly the same words as used originally.

Go to our website at
DRAG411.com
to locate any name listed
in any of the books
in our Ten Black Book series
and the details of each
book, entertainer,
and chapter.

Scoop
North America & Gay International Pageant Systems Merge
This is for the spouses of illusion. You may not know us, as we are the ones sitting quietly while our spouses show people "how it's done."
Legislative
DIVIDE AMONGST CAST
BAR
COMMUNITY CHEST
Confessions
My Virginity
DRAG Queen
EFFORTLESSLY
Fabulous

Before you build
an empire,
SPOTLIGHT
TODAY Magazine
Kings, Queens, FTM, MTF, Androgynous Performers, & Drag Show Promoters!
FTM
Community Chest
For every dollar you take from the public, return to the public in charity.

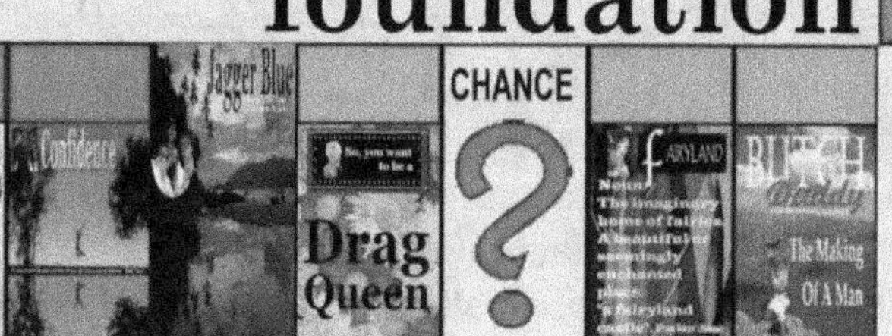
Stengthen your
foundation

Papier-mâché
Rest In Peace
Now Performing On A Grander Stage

Love, Sex, & Relationships
THE NAKED TRUTH

A Moment with Maggie
SPRING ISSUE
2012

Keeping it
SCHOOL

GO TO JAIL

Jagger Blue
Confidence
No, you want to be a
Drag Queen
CHANCE
?
FAIRYLAND
Noun:
The imaginary home of fairies. A beautiful seemingly enchanted place.
"a fairyland castle" - Fairy tales
BUTCH Daddy
The Making Of A Man
FREE
MAGAZINE

I am beginning to realize now, that there was something missing in me. I wasn't put together right. I was wounded. I still am, and I will probably have this empty part in me, until the day comes, that I will finally do as predicted, all those years ago, and go. I spent my entire adult life in search of something, something that I couldn't put my fingers on.

All of the outrageous antics that I was involved in. The acting out, the constant need for attention, the desperate need to be accepted, and liked. The drug addiction, alcoholism, and that overwhelming need for sex, that everyone talked about endlessly, with a never-ending stream of men, coming, and going... so many that I couldn't ever begin to remember them all. Some nights there were more than just one... Some nights, they were waiting in a line... I was insatiable.

From The Book Life Outside The Line by Gilda Golden
This is only a copy of the actual Magazine created in 2012.
Except for DRAG411.com, all email addresses and links
are no longer active or available.

Over 300 entertainers, columnists, photographers, and contributing writers, create the largest trade publication in history for Kings, Queens, FTM/MTF entertainers, androgynous performers, and drag show promoters. We will enter the page numbers at the end.

CONTENT

Drag Pets
May Trivia
Butch Daddy
Total Recall
Scoop
Vivikah's Jewelry Box
First Time
How Makanoe C's It
Drag Spouses Unite
Going Public
The Cameltoe Monologues
Out Of The Closet
Excited
Keeping It Old School
Another Moment with Maggie
Face On/ Face Off
The Naked Truth
Jagger Blue
Confidence
Fairyland
The Official Original Memorial
Confessions of a Drag Queen Photographer
So, You want to be a Drag Queen?
Effortlessly Fabulous
Legislative Update
Lipstick and Paint
June Trivia
The Next Ten
Oh Molly, By Golly!

This is only a copy of the actual Magazine created in 2012. Except for DRAG411.com, all email addresses and links are no longer active or available.

SPOTLIGHT TODAY Magazine is no longer in print.

"Moxie"
Performing Cher
From Candi Samples

**This is only a copy of the actual Magazine created in 2012.
Except for DRAG411.com, all email addresses and links
are no longer active or available.**

"Angel, Mojo,
& Sparky"

From Camille Sands

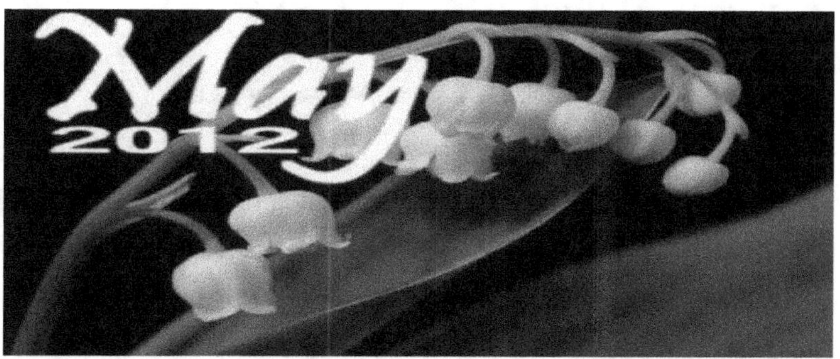

May Trivia

The photo above is one of the two flowers representing May. The beautiful woodland flowering plant, Lily of the Valley is poisonous. The second plant, the Hawthorne, tops the next page. It is actually an invasive weed in many countries, though popular in our country for hedges. The fruit is often made into jam. Use the following calendar to incorporate into your routines to stand out of the crowd.

    ❖   1st   May Day
    ❖   5th   Cinco de Mayo
    ❖   6th   National Teacher's Day
    ❖   8th   VE Day, World War II *
    ❖   13th   Mother's Day
    ❖   19th   Armed Forces Day -third Saturday
    ❖   24th   Victoria Day (Canada)
    ❖   28th   Memorial Day

Most people do not know this, but VE means Victory in Europe.

Month of May:

- ❖ Date Your Mate Month
- ❖ Foster Care Month
- ❖ National Barbecue Month
- ❖ National Bike Month
- ❖ National Blood Pressure Month
- ❖ National Hamburger Month
- ❖ National Photograph Month
- ❖ National Recommitment Month
- ❖ National Salad Month
- ❖ Older Americans Month

Weekly Celebrations in May:

- ❖ Nurse's Week - week one
- ❖ Wildflower Week - week two
- ❖ National Bike Week - week three
- ❖ National Police Week - week three
- ❖ Emergency Medical Services Week - week four

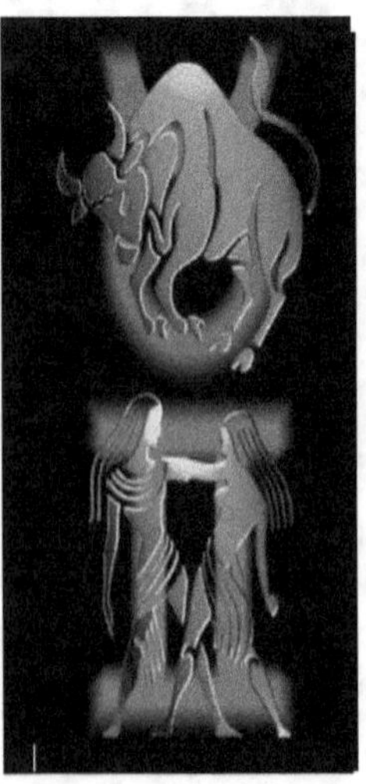

    Fifteen different birthstones mark the calendar month of May. The month defines the Sun/Star, Planetary, or Talismanic stones for the Zodiac sign of Taurus or Gemini. Two Zodiac signs span part of May. Birthstones for the calendar month of May are Emerald, Sapphire, Agate, and Carnelian. The Zodiac signs of Taurus and Gemini include 11 additional stones: Coral, Turquoise, Aventurine, Garnet, Amber, Rose Quartz, Tiger's Eye, Chrysoprase, Citrine, White Sapphire, and Pearl.

FROM THE EDITORS

I want to welcome you all to the Premiere Issue of SPOTLIGHT TODAY Magazine.

A HUGE Thank you to facebook, and to Publisher Todd Kachinski-Kottmeier for bringing this to life. I thank all of the contributors for their commitment and talent to get us off the ground at the speed of light. I also want to praise Coordinating Editor, Darlene House, for her unwavering commitment to collecting and organizing the pieces with our writers.

If you would like to become part of this project, please contact darlenehouse@bechavn.com.

We hope that you will find this, and our future issues, informative, poignant, and often humorous. We strive to bring you a top-quality quarterly magazine. We look forward to hearing from you.

ENJOY!!!

Steve Hammond
Senior Editor

Let me thank all of the people who contributed to SPOTLIGHT TODAY Magazine possible. By sharing your words as you have shared your talents with so many, you have brought this dream of Todd's to fruition. I have been proud to be a small part of this magnificent and generous undertaking and look forward to seeing this project continue to grow.

~Darlene House, Coordinating Editor

**This is only a copy of the actual Magazine created in 2012.
Except for DRAG411.com, all email addresses and links
are no longer active or available.**

BUTCH
Daddy
Your Ph.D from Germany
The Making
Of A Man
ButchDaddy@SpotlightTodayMagazine.com

There I sat in the back of my parent' s dark green Oldsmobile barreling down the interstate heading back to our simple home in Rochester. To this day, I can still hear the shrilling, sarcastic whine of my mother in the front seat, reprimanding my father.

"It takes more than balls to be a man." I glanced from the back seat as her words pierced the air into my father's ears. From around his headrest I could see his jowl line tense with each belittled word after another. He glanced at me. I could tell my father felt disparaged by her barrage of criticism, but speaking up would only complicate the situation.

What was I to say?

I was a twelve-year-old girl, sitting on the leather seat between a brother I could not stand, and an older sister that barely tolerated me in her life. The conversation carried on from the moment we left the church to the second my father escaped from the car into our old farmhouse. Surely, he was heading to the Frigidaire to pull out a cold can of Pabst Blue Ribbon.

"Men are pigs, "my mother tensely informed my sister. "Promise me Ruth, you won't mess with men until you are ready to find one that won't destroy your life."

"They all destroy your life," my sister replied. My brother Kal stared without emotion at a spot on the black plastic mat covering the floor in the car. "It's Beck you need to worry about."

Ruth tossed my name out there long enough for Kal to use it as a chance to escape from the car. He darted out, leaving the door open, with me sitting in the center, wondering how my name became part of the fit in the front seat. I hated the name Beck, or even Becky, but nobody seemed to care. My birth certificate said Rebecca, after my grandmother, but only she and I seemed to appreciate the bond.

"Are you having sex with boys?"

My mother's voice seemed to rise in both velocity and anger from a random comment tossed out by Ruth. I felt my legs starting to shake under the frilly undergarment poking from my dress.

"I've never even kissed a boy, Ruth is lying."

Ruth burst into laughter, "I never said she was having sex. I only hang with my girlfriends. Beck is always playing with the Barnhardt boys. If I didn't know better, I would think she was one of them."

"The Barnhart's wouldn't have her," my mother smiled at her own quip, opened the door, and left the car leaving Ruth sitting alone in the car with me.

"I didn't mean to tell her you want to be a damn Barnhart," Ruth whispered to me as she turned the chrome handle of the car. "I meant you want to be a boy. You are more of a boy than your own brother."

With that said, Ruth left the car, shutting the door, with me still perched on the hump of the center of the seat. A warm breeze gently rushed through the car and back out the door left open by Kal.

What did that comment mean?

Why did my mother scream, "It takes more than balls to be a man?"

In school we were taught that was exactly the meaning of being a man; I distinctly remember my grandmother pointing out the subtle difference between my brother and I... and that was one of the two dangly parts that made the grade.

Five years passed, and rarely a month went by without me thinking of those two conversations that took place on that summery Sunday afternoon. I eventually worked past the issues and complications posed to me in the backseat of the Cutlass, which now belonged to me in my senior year. I understood my mother's reprimand to my father, challenging his behavior and not his genitals. He passed away in my eleventh year of school, complications of untreated colorectal cancer. My brother took it hard, blaming my mother, God, and any random reason he could find. By the time Kal had time to graduate from high school, he was in prison for violently raping his girlfriend, and leaving her for dead near Broken Arrow creek.

My last month in school, I took Ellen's lead on television to come out of the closet to my family. My grandmother seemed challenged, but willing to work out the details. Ruth freaked and has not returned my calls, and my mother began speaking to me in this Zombie-form of facial expressions and calculated sentence structure. I made it easy for her, by telling her I was following my girlfriend to Kaiserslautern, Germany.

Christina was a year older than I was, and she entered the United States Army under the Don't Ask Don't Tell program. I did not have the slightest idea for a career, and now seemed let down that I chose to take Spanish in school as my foreign language. I signed up to start classes as a part-time student

Graduation went well, but my mother only went through the motions of having me in her life. I could see in her eyes the "Why can't you be like Ruth?" questions, hoping I would have mimicked my eldest sister by attending the university to meet a man, and have a couple of well-behaved grandchildren.

The following day, I went to the International Airport to depart, but only my grandmother came to see me off. My mother was unable to free herself from a Red Hat Society meeting of local women meeting at a Golden Corral near our home. I thought about it on the ten-hour flight across the Atlantic. "Maybe it was best she did not come." At least my grandmother's emotions were real, and did not portray a glimpse of disappointment and sorrow.

I would love to continue this story by telling you all the ways Christina and I rocked Kaiserslautern. It would have seemed so cool, but reality hits hard on a Private's military salary, joined by a partner struggling to find employment in a country where she "Spricht kein Deutsche." Within three months of my arrival, I found myself sleeping on the couch of a lesbian transformer, a male illusionist; something Americans refer to as Drag Kings.

It is hard to use the word drag in many of the bars in Europe as a generic heading, considering it literally means, "dressed as girl." Nothing about Kristin shouted "girl." She is to feminine, what a flower is to a black oil coated pipe wrench. We met her shopping in the big city at the local Aldi Süd; something Americans are now starting to become familiar with as Germany's "Aldi Grocery Stores."

Kristin is loud, but quickly became a more sophisticated character called, "Kristian" (Christian) when she performed across the country for the past three decades. This column is more about the lesson she shares with those she mentors. She has been my mentor for the past twelve years, and the eight parables she preaches are those that I shall share in each issue of SPOTLIGHT TODAY Magazine. The reason I selected this publication, is perhaps the reason many of us were brought on board, because Todd Kachinski-Kottmeier asked me to become part of it.

At no time in my life have I met this man, but many of us know his work. It ties so delicately to the first message I plan to discuss, because one of his quotes on facebook last year became many of the kings and male illusionists call to arms. It is the reason many of us are stepping up to take our due. He yelled at us with guilty pleasure,

"Act like a man!"

At first, I heard the shout of my mother's voice. I read the words on a facebook FTM (Female to Male) page, shared by one of his followers.

"Act like a man." What did this sentence mean, and why in hell would a man be telling me to act like a man?

I continued to read the note shared in the chat room. I did not save it word for word, but paraphrasing it will get the point across. Since Todd owns SPOTLIGHT TODAY Magazine, I am sure he will correct my errors at the end of the note, but I read the words as a lesbian. I shared them the past year with many performers, surprised so many agree with his stance. I hope that this magazine will be our calling card for the next generation.

"Act like a man," is based on the premise that men conquer. Compared to women as a whole, men have no problem taking what they desire; no matter if it belongs to them, no matter if it is fair, no matter who is hurt along the way. Not all men behave this way, but men in a generalized term. His conversation followed the original release of his popular book, *Official Drag Handbook*, with Steve Hammond. Todd remarked that an invitation was sent openly across facebook for men and women to participate in the ground breaking book, but only one female entertainer stepped up to the plate, while hundreds of men stumbled over each other to post their comments.

You can tell Mr. KK (or whatever you Americans call him), was crushed by the low turnout of participating male illusionists. He went on a justified rampage, and along the way made many of us look in the mirror at ourselves differently, as he pointed out to all of us for being so critical to "drag queens" constantly stealing the light, leaving us to stumble upon the breadcrumbs of entertainment bookings and media attention.

"You need to act like a man, and take what is yours."

What a great first issue concept for all of us to take away. RuPaul is not letting us be on her show. Few international stages are open to us. Here is this American publisher constantly begging us to "let him" publicize us for free, and twelve days later, he is posting comments about the sounds of crickets coming from our community.

Put a dress on a man, and he becomes a caricature of what he perceives us to be as women, but he is still a man. I believe this confidence, created subconsciously from generations of aggressiveness cultivated in our society, bolsters their resolve to be noticed. In the back rooms, women demand recognition equally on stage, but battle their own insecurities and anger when challenged to step up to the plate. We are either claiming to be too busy to change the course of our future, for not only us, but also those following quickly behind us, around us, and because of us. We are shouting so loudly that we are pissed, that we fail to hear the timid voices of those struggling to catch our attention, and to help open the door for us (not that I believe Todd is quiet or timid in person).

We cannot change tomorrow. Mom is right, "men are pigs."

I happen to like bacon, so therefore, I will gladly pretend to be them on stage, but more importantly, I need to take their cue off stage and steal the spotlight. I refuse to wait my turn for attention long overdue. I am personally going to contact the females that dress to impress as men and ask them to get involved with this magazine. No, I will not be asking them... I will be demanding they help start the march for us, for the parade starts here, and we will not become equal as long as we insist we are victims. We will not become equal if we let people speak for us in a venue open to all of us. We will not become equal until we all stand together to be noticed, to find value, to ensure our presence is marked in history one word at a time.

Dee Gregory and PurrZsa Kyttyn
TOTAL RECALL

In 2010, The Official Drag Handbook asked the first of 102 questions that would later become the groundbreaking project, the Official Drag Handbook setting world records for the craft. The responses, over 255,000 words, could not be placed in a single book. A portion of each issue of SPOTLIGHT TODAY Magazine will be used to reprint most of the comments for each question. This was question one.along with new responses all of you place on our Official facebook page.

My First Time!
When was the first time dressed in the opposite sex?

Note: Comments edited lightly.

These are the actual conversations placed by fellow male and female entertainers in 2010. It is also important to note that many of them later confessed to "being pretty fucked up" when they filled out the questionnaire. Some of these contributors are no longer alive, but their hearts we share in the notes below.

Michael Wilson
Back up for Stephanie Scott at the Power Company of Durham. She did *The Lord Is Trying To Tell You Something*. I stole the choir robes from the church across the street. (Yes, they were returned)

Deva DaVyne
The first time I dressed up was back in middle school. I was home alone and went into my mother's closet and decided to play dress up. I remember my mom walking in on me, wearing her clothes and high heels. All she told me was that if I scuffed her floor she would scuff my butt.

Naomi Wynters
I was young, around nine years old; it was for a play we were putting on. Someone had to play the old lady. To me it was nothing,. just a role in the play, so I thought nothing of it.

Stephen Brooks
I played a nun in a school play...is a habit considered a dress?? It was a dress to me... I felt sooooo pretty!!

Felina Cashmere
My mother use to dress me as a girl with my sister, so I blame her. She grew my hair out and everyone would comment on her two "beautiful "daughters. But, as a "drag queen," it was around the age of 15 for St. Patrick's Day.

Amanda Love
Around age 4 I think. My mom has pictures of me with my pink GEM (a cartoon from the 80's) guitar, her silk slip a boa and heels. I guess she should have known then.

**This is only a copy of the actual Magazine created in 2012.
Except for DRAG411.com, all email addresses and links
are no longer active or available.**

Liza and Vincent Wiercinski Darcelle's XV in Portland Oregon
Photo credit: Glenn W. Storm.

Candy Cane, Jennifer Justice, and Stefani Cole
Photo Credit: Mimi Welch

Maxine Padlock

From the age of 10 all I could do was imagine, but the first time I actually put on a dress I was 33 years old ... I am 45 now - and they said I wouldn't make 21. That goes with my story of being at The Avenue for plus size women. I got dressed for Halloween in a very nice gold and flashy outfit. I think there are pics in my profile.

Daphne Ferraro
Probably 4 or 5, but as I recall it was more of a leotard and sheer curtain combo. I think I was 6 when I sported my first one piece swimsuit. It was leopard and yellow. I saw it sitting on my bed and I had to wear it! I pranced around the pool in front of my family, my brother, and a few of his friends.

Mike Asterman:
It was in 1968. I was working at the club above the Victory Theater on Main Street in Dayton

Selina Kyle
I didn't know about it, but my Mom had a picture of me riding an old cast iron tricycle, in my Grandma's heels, house coat and oh yeah...that's right, a Sunday hat twice my size, when I was about 5. According to her, I did it all the time.

Diamond Dunhill
1998 was the year. Two best friends (at the time) decided to dress-up for Halloween, doing it as a group thing. We entered as many As 3 or 4 contests that night as The Yeast Inspection Gurlz (I was Meredith Monistat, along With Dyna Lotrimin and Fiona Femstat). We won The Early Bird Contest!

Babette Schwartz
 I was four years old; there is a picture of me wearing a half-slip and pearls while twirling around the front yard.

Misty Eyez
When I was 10 years old I used to wear my Sisters FULL CIRCLE SKIRT (so when you spin it goes all the way out) and my Mothers BRA and stuff it full of Toilet Paper... RUN around the house in her HEELS and SINGING OUT LOUD, not Lip syncing to the headphones on repeat of Madonna's I AM A MATERIAL GIRL .... I did it sooo often I kept getting caught, and my mother threw away my sisters skirt even though it was both hers and my fave

Kiki LaFlare Santangilo
I put on my first dress my Sophomore year of college. I started watching RuPaul's Drag Race on LOGO and thought, "Hey, I love makeup, I love performing...I think I can do that!" I put on a dress, did my makeup, put on a wig, slipped on
some heels, and never looked back :)

Adrian Leigh
I was 16 and my then GIRL friend dressed me for Halloween. I was a girl and she was a guy ...the rest is history .. From coming out as a gay man to competing for titles locally.

Anastasia Fallon
Hahaha, actually...when I was 3 years old. My Aunt was watching me for the night, and we started playing in her closet. I don't know whether or not my sister was there, but I do know that my Aunt had the only copy of a picture of me strutting in her heels & one of her wonderfully loud, shoulder padded, 80's cocktail dresses.

Champagne T. Bordeaux
I was nineteen years old, believe it or not... I lost a bet I could win the talent contest without a dress and or wig, well I lost that bet not once, but twice... the rest is his-tory.

Mis Sadistic
I was 5 years old, it was in kindergarten class. I was playing dress up with some of my classmates. I put on a dress, hat and girls shoes. What I remember most was the frightening reaction from the teacher and the others around me. I was scared by them!

Patricia Mason
I was about 4 or 5 going through an old trunk in the grandparent's shed with my sister. We did a fashion show and I don't remember much, but everyone thought it was cute then...in high school and beyond however, not so much.

Lady Tajma Hall
I was 3 and my mother put me in the dress! She found this cute pink and white dress that looked like a jumper and thought it would look amazing on me! She bought the dress, put me in the dress and put my hair in two ponytails with matching pink bows! She knew that I was a girl and wanted to help me realize it!

Jade Shanell
I was 33 years old, and we always had a Halloween contest where I worked. Well that year, since I loved drag queens so much, I decided I would dress as one that day. I came in 8 inch Bordello shoes, blue glittered

dress, makeup and hair that reached to God, and big jewelry that shines and glittered so much that Tinkerbell would be jealous that it gave her dust competition honey and well let's say, that is when Lady was born and the rest was history sugar. They all loved it and I have been enjoying it ever since.

The Original Cover of The Official DRAG Handbook

Kori Stevens
I was 26 years old. It was Halloween at the Parliament House in Orlando, FL. I was dating someone who was good friends with Darcel Stevens, and it was his idea that I go out in Drag for Halloween, I spent WAY TOO MUCH MONEY to look a hot mess, but had an amazing time, and even won some money for it.

Vivika D'Angelo
I was 6 months old. My mom dressed me up in my cousins baptismal dress I told her, "See, you started me at an early age," but I would have to say I was 7 years old; I was bored, my mom was cooking, and dad was working. I went into her room, put on heels, a dress, and lipstick. I came out and said, "What do you think?" She laughed and said ummm that shade of lipstick is not you

Kier
I was about 4 or 5, my mum actually bought a dress I fancied so I tried it on and safety pinned it so it was tight on me

Toni DaVyne
I was about 13. My sister had to wear a dress for a family function and threw a fit about wearing it, so being the queen that i am, I told her she could wear my pants and I would take over the dress. Oh you should have seen the look on my uncle's and father's faces! I got my butt tore up after, but it was worth it

Amy DeMilo
I was around 5 or 6 the first time I dressed in my sister's clothes. Even sometimes I'd go to one of my friend's house, who use to take dance classes. I'd dress up in her ballet costumes and parade around her house...

Michelle Tatum
I was 6 years old. Me and my sister used to play "HOUSE." I was always the MOM . I would wear this little skirt and a halter top ...my father would always "CATCH" us and tell me to take it off ...

Shealita BaBay
I'm not a Boy I'm a god damn woman! Sent by White Lord Jesus

Conundrum
I was about 12. I did it for Halloween. I guess, in my mind, it was the perfect time to do it because on Halloween no one would really judge me for doing so. I remember opening the door to trick-or-treaters, and of course it was people I went to school with. Surprisingly, they were only slightly amused.

Naomi D-Lish
I was in full drag on Halloween when i was 12. Skirt, heels and boobs to boot. My mother did my makeup and restyled the store wig we bought. It was fun, but it was more satirical at the time because I was still convinced I was straight back then

Stephanie Roberts
I was about 19 and it was on Halloween. Later that night my parents found a paper where I had written down everything I was wearing and who I borrowed it from. They knew then what my costume was, and I had a lot of explaining to do when I got home.

Barbra Herr
6 or 7...got gussied up in Mom's wedding dress and fell asleep...when Mom got home the junk hit the fan...

Katrina Starr
One month before my first show, my sister and I were practicing my face and I put on my mother's clothes. We laughed and cried, then my mom showed up; so i threw the clothes off shoved my make up in my bag, and ran to the shower

Wendy G Kennedy
I was 12 years old and my mom beat the living daylights out of me... I did it after I watched an episode of Bugs Bunny on the TV... I mean I used her makeup, dress, and heels and one of her wigs, I must say I looked rather cute in those garments... I`m blessed to have similar features of my mom and even my feet kinda look like hers too.

Beverly LaSalle
The earliest I can recall putting on a dress would be around 5 years old when I was playing house with the girls in the Catholic nursery school I attended. Needless to say, I went to public school after that.

Jade Jolie
I was around 5 or 6 and my female cousins would stuff me in my one pant leg of pajama pants like a tube top mermaid dress, and sing part of *Your World* from *The Little Mermaid*. Drag was inevitable

Tabatha Lovall
I must have been about 5. My sister and I used to put on Tiffany concerts. We would dress up and lip-sync. I loved it!

Jami Micheals
I was oh around 12 years old and it wasn't a dress. It was actually a pair of my mom's brown suede knee high boots. I lived for those things. She would go to the grocery store and I would prance around the house in them with the music cranked up

LeAnna Love
Seven, and it was for trick or treating.

Dmentia Divinyl
I was 12. I tried on my mom's brassiere and her high heels and a slip and some fake pearls with lipstick. BOY did I look like A girl trapped in a man's bod!

Alanna Divine
I was 15 years old. I had watched a Mae West movie and thought damn this bitch is getting all the attention. So I went and found my mother's evening gown and put it on with her heels....ugh! The definition of the word "hot mess"

Geraldine Queencabaret
I was four, and I'd play innocently with the old dresses my mom would give to my sisters to play with. But, when I was 23 I'd wait for everybody (my 2 sisters and 2 brothers) to occasionally leave the apartment we were living in. I'd lock the door and shut all the windows and put my sister's little black dress and a nice scarf on my head (my sisters didn't needed a wig) and go see myself in the mirror and cry for a long time. I was feeling great, but the reflection I'd see was too much for me to bear. Once I was out of tears, I had to put the dress and scarf back in place, open all the windows and unlock the door, and start being strong again until the next time I'd be alone. It's not a nice cute story, but the beginning of something fantastic isn't always nice and cute :)

Vegas Platinum
I remember putting on my mom's heels when i was 10 or 11, but not any of her clothes... the dress waited for me actually to start doing drag!

Angela Dodd
I was 21 and in the Army, stationed at Fort Bragg, NC. I didn't dress up in women's clothes as a child. I was a rocker, HS class of 1992. Poison, Crue, Jovi, Warrant, Queen, Aerosmith, etc. However, what I did do is dress up as my rock idols and put on a make believe concert in our basement. I'd pull my t-shirt up over my head so the neck became my hairline and the rest of the shirt acted as my rocker hair that I could head bang with. That is pretty close to drag, don't you think. I'm so glad I never got caught in all my femme rocker glory!

Brandon M. Caten
I was 18 and wanted to help raise money by entering a "Womanless Beauty Pageant," and while all of the other boys didn't take it seriously, I had to look stunning! Needless to say, I won the crown, and there was born Chanel LaCoudre

Alisa Summers
For me, it was never a dress. I was all about shoes. Whether it was my mother's or my grandmothers', I was all about some heels. There are pictures of me as a child, probably around 4 years old, in heels and hats. I'm sure if you ask my mother, she'd be more than happy to share them :)

Jeffrey Powell
I remember it was in elementary school, probably about the time I was in 4th or 5th grade, for a Halloween festival. I had on a yellow dress and white heels ...nobody recognized who I was...I was kinda glad though cause I didn't want to go in a dress. It was my mom's idea. The second time was just a few months ago...and this time I enjoyed it :)

Demonica da Bomb
I was 18 and asked to perform at JR's

Juwana Jackson
I was about 7 years old. I would run around the neighborhood pretending to be She Ra, screaming "I AM SHE-RA" I used my dad's long t shirt with a belt around the waist as the dress, my towel as a wig, and my dad's socks with ABC blocks duct taped to the bottom of them as boots.

Crystal Belle
I was in Preschool. My friend, Tara, constantly fought me over who would be mom when we played house. I naturally wanted to wear the sequin dress, and she was the one wearing her normal clothes. Dress up was fun and innocent then, so no one thought anything about it. The funny thing was I always wanted to wear high heels too. I guess I've always been born to wear heels, it just feels natural.

Esme Russell
I was around 8 years old. My mom left me home babysitting my little brother, and I put on her high heels and one of her dresses.

Lacey Lynn Taylors
The first time I remember dressing as a "female," my siblings and cousins were playing school. I was the oldest, so I got to be the teacher, but "Teachers are girls!" I said. My aunt then gave me a dress and lipstick and a pair of high heels, and that's what started it all.

PurrZsa Kyttyn
I had to have been around 8 or so and it was one of my sister's. I remember always thinking she had cuter clothes than me. On Halloween, I went dressed up in my sister's brownie outfit and her Pocahontas dress!

Eunyce Raye
I was in middle school and went as an old lady one year

Joey Brooks
There was a talent show at the El Goya in Tampa, Florida. Brenda Dee, the show director, suggested that I make my magic act unique by doing it in Drag. Not only did I win the show, but it changed the direction of my life. I feel strange replying to all of these questions, that I'll be discussing in great detail in my new book, "Joey Brooks; The Show Must Go On". <Click this comment to read part of Joey's book.>

Glitz Glam
I was probably 8 or 9 when I started putting on my Mom's Bra, using water balloon's as tits. I loved wearing her shoes as well. She had one pair of special Black Velvet & Gold 4-inch spikes I loved wearing. However, by 11 or so my Fred Flintstone toes wouldn't fit in them anymore:(I didn't start wearing dresses until my early teens. My cousin had a FABULOUS wardrobe!)

Mis Sadistic and Amanda Lay
Official Drag Handbook

Shawn Kelly
When I was little and living in the Farm town of Mt Home, Idaho. My mother dressed me as Sarah from *Hocus Pocus*. I was a little sad because I wanted to be Winifred... I was a hit.

Afeelya Bunz
Age 29, I did it to help a friend with fundraisers

Teri Courtney (RIP)
My mom told me I used to wear her skirts as a lil boi, and how funny it was. It wasn't so funny at 16 when I was growing breasts!!

Lady Liemont
Probably around 17, when i started to become a Club kid, thanks to a very special performer by the name of Adrian Androgyny....Love her to death. But truly didn't start wearing full wigs until about 10 years later when I crossed over to full fishy drag...

Patrice Knight:
I was 15 and I decided to play dress up in my Stepmother's closet. I pulled out a pretty dress and her high heels and paraded around the house before my parents got home.

Raven Manniac
I was 5 of 6 and liked to put on the clothes in my Grandma's attic. I had to promise not to tell my Mom and Dad so they wouldn't get mad...

Jade Daniels
Since I grew up mostly with my father, I never really had dresses just laying around at my disposal. So unfortunately, It wasn't until my sophomore year of high school, when I was 15 years old. I was in the Drama Club (SHOCKER), and we did ...a comical version of "Twas The Night Before Christmas" in front of the whole school, and I was one of the "Sugar Plum Fairies" that danced in their heads. It was essentially 4 boys dressed up in the marching band's Color Guard uniforms. The next year I was in a Cheerleading skirt doing a cheer routine at a Pep Rally...

Raquel Payne
I was like 10 when I first put on a dress. Of course it belonged to my mother and dragged the ground, with teal green pumps that I don't believe could ever match a thing in anyone's closet. I danced around to the sounds on the radio. I felt like a princess.

TotiYanah Diamond
I was 5 or 6. It was my mom's. I loved putting on her dresses, makeup and heels and walking around when i thought no one was looking. I had so much fun with the jewelry and everything. At that age I didnt know how to put on makeup. I knew I looked a mess, but I had fun!

Monique Michaels
I really don't remember ever putting on a dress when I was younger, but I do remember the first time I put on high heels. I was 5 and my mother had what were, to me, the most beautiful Italian shoes. I asked her how she walked in them, and she had me put them on and walk.

Jaeda Fuentes
The very first time I ever put on a dress was when I was 5. I used to always love walking around in my mom's clothes and her cowboy boots. She used to always walk in and find me rummaging through her closet, when I told her I did drag for the first time it's no wonder why she wasn't surprised.

Scoop
North America International
North America &
Gay International
Pageant Systems
Merge
AmandaLav
@SpotlightTodayMagazine.com

During the Miss Gay International at Large this past November, the announcement of this new merger was given for North America and Gay International. The newly crowned, Londenn D Raine's new title was not Gay International but the newly merged North America International.

Scott Stebane, owner of the North America Pageant System, and Dena Cass, owner of Gay International Pageant System decided to merge creating a stronger system to thrive. Stebane is creating plans for the new and improved pageant system to take a spin from the current top pageant systems, but with its own unique twist.

Miss Gay North America International 2011, Neely O'Hara said, "What makes this pageant unique is the avant-garde fashion category."

This avant-garde fashion category is one of five for the Miss Divisions of the new pageant system. The male division's unique category is "Club Wear."

Stebane said there are two things that inspired him to create this new system, "Having been a promoter for another system, I saw how promoters where treated, I felt the pageant should have gone in a different direction. I created the new system to also take care of the promoters. I wanted this pageant system to be about the entertainers' talent, but also their charity work. We plan for this new system to work with many charities to give back to the community."

According to the North America International website their mission is

1. To provide a wide-range of quality entertainment choices to our audiences,
2. To provide an alternative pageant system to entertainers that truly encompasses the diversity of the GLBT community, and
3. To give back to the community in the form of charitable contributions to GLBT-based organizations."

North America International Board member Jazmine Roberts said "I hope to see this pageant grow to representatives each states before moving internationally."

Alisa Summers and My'Chryl Purr

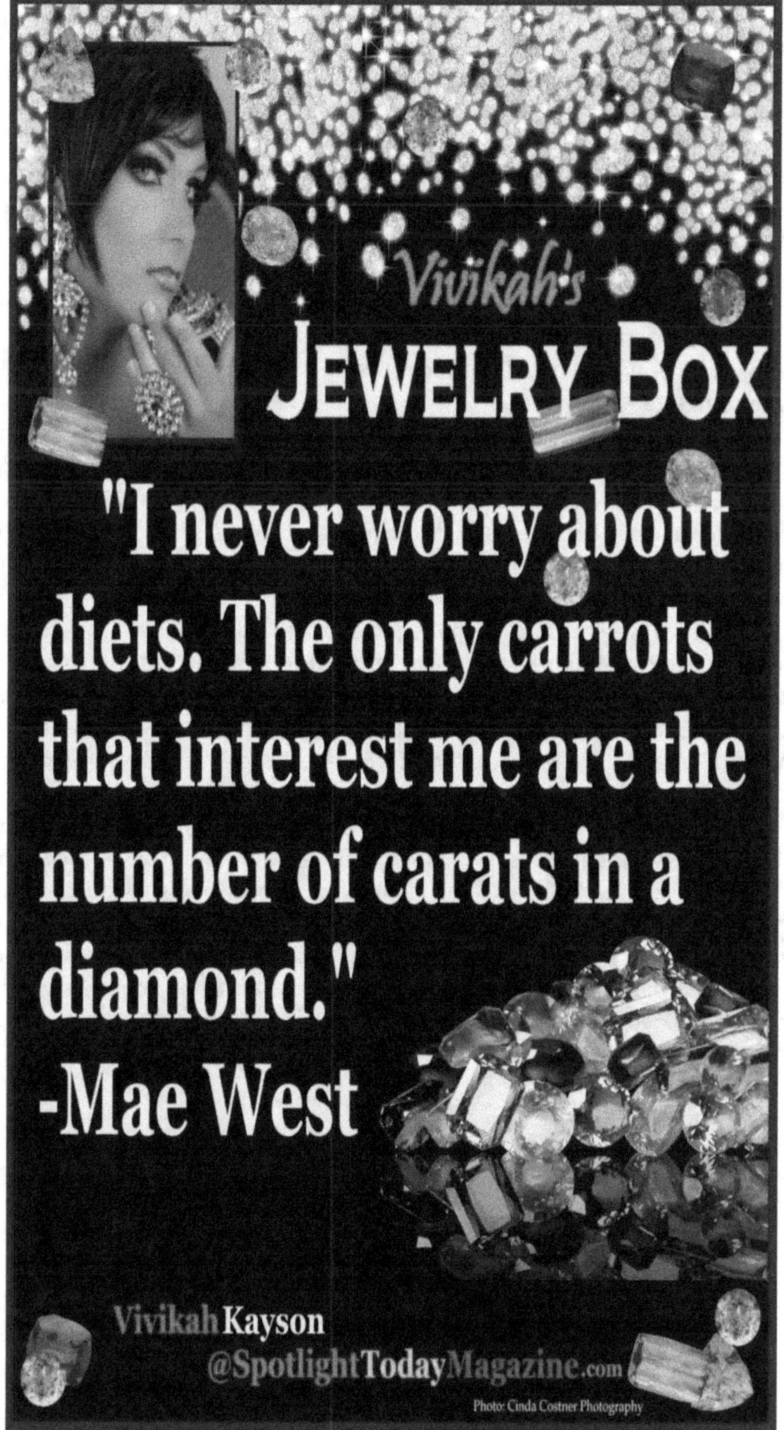
Vivikah's
JEWELRY BOX
"I never worry about diets. The only carrots that interest me are the number of carats in a diamond."
-Mae West
Vivikah Kayson
@SpotlightTodayMagazine.com
Photo: Cinda Costner Photography

Every entertainer collects favorite parts of costuming. The items accentuate their outfits for pageants, performances, or simply for socializing around the bar. Some enjoy shoes and wigs, but the absolute most fabulous little things that anyone can accumulate is JEWELS!

Jewels can come from anywhere. When competing in a pageant, I recommend nice, well made, "drag" jewels. There are many amazing people in business creating absolutely stunning custom designed pieces. This can get costly very fast however. Most entertainers, especially in the beginning, cannot afford to jump right into this side of jewelry collection. A great way to start is places such as groups on facebook, where entertainers are selling, or trading items. Buy them at lower prices because they have been worn, or may need a little repair work, which is usually inexpensive to have completed.

Antique shops, thrift stores, and garage sales are a fun place to find great pieces. You can find some amazing things for a little or nothing. This is a great way to build a collection for the entertainer with comedy skits. Old beads, plastic jewelry, broaches, and things of this nature are in abundance at these places. One of my favorite bracelets came from a thrift shop, and it is probably thirty years old.

I have attempted to make jewelry and failed horribly. If anyone wants to attempt it, go for it. I have decided to leave to the professionals. Buy giant hoop earrings, drops, wide necklaces, and bracelets from a more cost efficient store, and embellish them with stones is a great idea for shows. I have had some success with this, except for the little burns from a hot glue gun and gluing two fingers together with E6000.

By using your imagination, you can make creative and fun pieces with endless possibilities. I would not recommend these pieces in pageantry. I created pieces using gluing stones but they showed crackling on the backs or got hazy once the glue dried. This also depends on what type of stones are used, and this will be addressed in later issues of SPOTLIGHT TODAY Magazine, but you do not want to be competing for a crown and have the spotlight on and those baubles not SPARKLE!

When was the first time you decided you liked dressing up as the opposite sex?
Tell us your age and your cute story around it.

Papi Chulo

The first time I put on clothes that were strictly the opposite sex was when I decided to climb a tree in our front yard. I was 7 and my mom made me wear a dress that day. I felt awkward from the minute she put me in the dress. I believe the dress only lasted on my body for about five minutes. I ran into my brother's room, who is only a year older than me, and I took his boxers and his shorts and shirt put them on and went outside and climbed a tree! A few minutes later my mom came outside to check on me and thought I was my brother . She went inside and called my name and I screamed I'm outside MOMMMM! She ran back outsdie and said I should have known. I found my new skin. That is where I have remained the rest of my life! Papi Chulo was born. I have always bought clothes of the opposite sex. I feel comfortable in them, and wear them daily. Now when Papi Chulo dresses up, that is a different story. There is sex appeal and drives the femmes crazy....not to mention, I turn heads. I am always looking for ways to make Papi Chulo..... Suave!!

Butt Wiser

I was 6 when I started playing dress up. I got in my friend's parents' closet and he got in his mom's clothes and I got in his dad's. I drew a mustache and beard on with his mom's eye shadow. It was hilarious.

Angel Khaos

I was 22 years old and in the GLBT bar for the very first time. I saw a crown on the wall and inquired; to my surprise I learned that it was for a drag contest. I was drunk and thought it would be funny to do-- so I ran...WON, and 2 months later won another title. Here I am, 10 years later, and my creativity is THRIVING. I JUST won the First Ever Mr Trexx MI (Male Impersonator) title, I am running for Syracuse Gay Pride, and on my way to competing for a NATIONAL Title, ALL from doing drag. I can't thank the people who got me started ENOUGH for all that I have accomplished.

Cathy Craig

I was actually 14. I went out as a girl on Halloween with my sisters and the cab driver tried to pick me up, scared the heck out of me. But, the first time regularly was the 2nd time I was in a gay bar, JJ's in Cleveland Ohio. I went there with a friend and saw men on stage moving their lips to women's songs. **B**eing an actor, I said I can do that, so off to Lane Bryant I went. My first drag name was Lorain. That is where I lived, Lorain Ave. But to my luck it was changed by my drag mother and another entertainer, Big Mama, to Cathy Craig.

Horchata
13, I was out in the desert and threw a sheet around me and was just playing around like I was in a bar talking to people. No one saw (I hope), I WAS A MESS. I wore my mother's shoes and I just seemed to glide in them.

Naomi Wynters
I was about 21. I didn't think I could be a performer, but i had a full team helping me get ready. I was quite content with the results, as well as the ability to actually pull off being a woman.

Deva DaVyne
14. I would come home and raid my mother's closet. I would always enjoy playing with her makeup and putting on some Gloria Estefan and dance around the house. I would always get sad when I had to take it all off before she got home.

Felina Cashmere
I was 15 and it was for St. Patrick's Day at school. Seeing as my heritage is Irish, I figured "why not?" Red wig and all. My father never found out, thank G-d.

Maxine Padlock
I had no clue - and I am actually writing this in my book I am working on about growing up and being bullied. But my earliest memory was when Wonder Woman came out in the 70's and I loved doing that twirl in my robe - but I liked to make believe it was a dress and I loved putting on my mother's high heels too.

Amanda Bone
I was dared to enter a talent contest at a club, and I just liked it. Even though I didn't win, I came back

Selina Kyle
I was 17. I had a friend dress me up and put me in makeup, because he was more experienced than I was. We went to a bar, and I learned that doing cheap drag...makes you look and feel cheap, now I know that it takes a lot of money to look that cheap.

Misty Eyes
I did it from 9 - 12 and used to WISH I was a girl, constantly putting towels on my head and pretending it was my LONG HAIR...Even went to school in drag in 4th grade for Halloween..... but then got really Christian and didn't do it again till after my senior year of college (21), also for Halloween... and that was when I knew I had to be a queen

Diamond Dunhill

I was 20, according to MySpace/facebook. With countless friends/future drag colleagues who painted me when I wanted, so I could go out and "Be Pretty". I didn't do my makeup and was afraid to go for TWO YEARS! But, it was cool and I was quickly recognized, as I gradually went out more often as "Diamond Dunhill."

If your name is not on these postings, go to our site and get involved before June 12, 2012. at: Drag411.com

Miss Gigi

Well, it was at work. One year we all decided that the men would dress as women, and all the women as men for Halloween....needless to say I was the only one who dressed up. I had hair down to my calves, and my mom did my make-up. I looked like a orangi...sh hooker.....it was something. I had fish net stockings on, and a short dress that barely covered my butt. They all got a kick out of it. I even went to the extent to Nair my legs...big mistake! When you're putting it on, and it gets close to the "twins" - talk about a hot package for a lil bit. I was about 21.

Makanoe

I guess I have always liked dressing up as a female. If you're wanting an age, I can remember as young as 4 years old trying to walk in my mother's pumps. Barbie and my Mother were my first inspirations to wear high heels, and because I started wearing pumps at such a young age, I can sprint in some 6 inch platforms bitches! I guess it didn't help my mother let my hair grow to my waist till her crazy boyfriend at the time shaved me bald at age 3.5!

Diedra Windsor Walker

I am currently 35 years old, and I have been doing female impersonation for four years. I am a cancer survivor, and also had the fortune to live and know Norma Kristie...the original Miss Gay America. Anyways, after my bout with cancer I was bemoaning how the cancer took a toll on my body. Norma suggested I try the art of female impersonation. At first I said, "OH I COULDN'T," but I warmed to the idea and came out at Halloween and tried it. I liked it so much, I competed for Miss Gay Little Rock, America in a few months. I came in dead last, but I caught the dream of being a female impersonator. I slowly worked on my character, got help from my sisters. In four years, I have won titles in three different systems, and am a title in the Imperial Court System for the realm of All Alaska. I have performed in Anchorage, Alaska to the famous Stonewall Inn in New York City. I am a successful promoter for three years and I have four drag sons. None of them do drag, but all four (who are gay) call me Mom and they are my sons.

Amanda Love
I guess it was after that first time seeing a show, thinking I can do that

Adrian Leigh
It all started as a way to get into the bars. At that time drags were not usually carded upon entry - i did it to gain entry as a "walk -around" queen. Eventually, I was old enough, I started entering competitions

Anastasia Fallon
That came around the time I was in High School. At the end of each year, our Thespian Troupe would host "The Mason Awards" (named for our teacher). My junior year, a friend and I decided to perform one of the new hot songs..."The Boy Is Mine" by Brandy & Monica. When I heard the cheering that night, I realized the power that illusion has on an audience. Even then, when it was done poorly...

Champagne T. Bordeaux
I can't say I ever liked it, i just needed the outside world to relate to me the way I could understand, that was age 7. The drag of it all became enjoyable around the age of 20, when I won Miss Gay Columbus America.

Mis Sadistic
I was 15 years old. I was at the Ice Palace on Fire Island. I saw Connie Francis coming across the deck. At the time, I was mesmerized by this man who looked just like her. I stayed for the drag show, they used to have one every Sunday. I was so lost in the moment, I didn't realize how much time went by. I had missed the last ferry home. I was busy talking with the showgirls. That was a defining moment in my life. I knew then I wanted to be a Drag Queen.

If your name is not on these postings, go to our site and get involved before June 12, 2012. at: Drag411.com

Patricia Mason
In early high school, when I was left alone, I would sneak into my sister's room and put on her clothes, and even one time walked out of the house dressed like her. No one ever knew or found out. I guess I just liked being someone different.

Lady Tajma Hall
As I mentioned in the first question, my mother put me in a dress at the age of 3 and I loved it! I continued to wear dresses as long as my mother would put me in them. If I was not in a dress, I was in a cute pastel jumper, always with matching bows on my ponytails!

Jocelyn Summers
I have always felt a little girly. Even as a boy I get called ma'am a lot. People think I am a lesbian. I first started getting into it in 1996, after seeing some shows in Tampa, and I thought I want to do that! I had always wanted to be a singer and be on stage. I realized early I didn't have the voice for it. Jocelyn hit the scene. I was addicted.

Jade Shanell
I think it was when I first dressed up in drag for Halloween at work, and everyone enjoyed it at work. A different personality came out of me and I just loved it, and loved seeing how others around me enjoyed it.

Kori Stevens
I knew when I was just a wee little boy. I was a latch-key child, and when I would get home from school, I would go into my parent's room and play in my mother's closet, trying on and prancing around in all her good things - WITHOUT MAKE-UP.......!!!!

Brianna Lee
I liked it to a point. I received my first credit card at 16 for the store called 16+, before Layne Bryant was the big girls' store. I liked the fact that my baby face back in 19 blah blah blah was easy to paint, and become feminine. My co-workers back then saw my audition video for the Putting On The Hits audition, and said WOW, what legs!!! I felt at that age I knew it all. (Of course I was wrong)

Vivika D'Angelo
I was 22yrs old, and decided to go to a club in Mexico and see the drag show there. I dressed up along with my best friend. When we got there, they looked at us and said, "Very cute, but if you do this you will look even better."

Kier
I was doing a home-made horror movie with some friends when i was 12-14. My drag name at that time was Madame Suicide

Toni DaVyne
I've always loved dressing like a girl! Even as a toddler I always hated wearing loose fitting clothes, and I yelled at my mother when she tried putting corduroys on me

Jessica Jade
The first time I did it and enjoyed it, was when I was 19 for Halloween. Me and my lesbian roomie decided to go as each other. When I got hit on by a drunk hot frat boy, I decided that this was fun! :)

Amy DeMilo
I've been dressing up since I was a kid, always in my sister's or mom's makeup and clothes.

Michelle Tatum
The first time i decided I LIKED dressing up was when i could actually go out as my drag persona and pass as a girl... I was like 15.

If your name is not on these postings, go to our site and get involved before June 12, 2012. at: Drag411.com

Pandora DeStrange
I loved playing Sonny and Cher as a child...I was always Cher of course!

Shealita BaBay
When I got sick and tired of HOMOSEXUALS, GOD Damn LIBERALS!

Conundrum
I started wearing female clothing on a regular basis when I was in my teens. I used to wear my best friend's clothes all the time. I know at one point I had more of her clothes then my own!

Lisa Carr
Drag isn't about dressing up like a female for me. It's about putting on a show with an incredible illusion. I've always liked performing, but as a female impersonator, I can be the creative director, producer, and star!

Katrina Starr
Well, I did it for a school fundraiser for Haiti. I never really thought of doing it before, but after that first number, when the audience clapped and cheered, all the awkwardness went away. It was like I was just in another play, there was nothing weird anymore. From that point on I liked doing what i do.

Wendy G Kennedy
Well, I always thought girls get all the fun, and they have better and more colorful gear than men. I was 12 years old when I put on my mom's clothes, but I got the living tar beat out of me. I made the decision to become a Drag Queen after I was asked to play as a Drag Queen for a

Movie in March 2010, when I did my research. I decided to give it my best shot. We only live once ya know?

Beverly LaSalle
The first time I decided I enjoyed dressing as a female was the first time I was on stage. I was 17 years old, and had been doing drag, and going out to the bars. I had the honor of becoming friends with Dana Douglas, a

former Miss Florida (among many other titles) and was invited to do a guest spot during her show. Once I walked out onto the stage, and the spotlight hit me, I knew I had found my calling!

Jade Jolie
My senior year in High School my friends and I had a project in film class to remake a music video into our own parody. We chose Lady Marmalade and Christina. It was just too hard to pass up at the time.

Jami Micheals
I actually started when i was 19 years old, a little late by most standards, but my now ex bf hung out in the female impersonator community and he just assumed that he could do makeup by association. Not true. I looked a mess, but you couldn't tell me any different at the time.

Dmentia Divinyl
At 15, I dressed up as a sexy old lady for Halloween. I used two plush Pac-Man dolls as boobs and I wore a nighty and a grey curly wig, I think it made me feel like I had a lot of balls, so it made me feel sexy to do it. I actually went to school dressed like that for Halloween, too!

Geraldine Queencabaret
When I was 24 years old I decided to follow my heart. I told my sister that I thought I wasn't just a gay guy. It was deeper than that, and I asked her to help me, encouraging me, and me not repressing myself anymore.

Angela Dodd
I liked it from day one, at Keri Nichols home, when Keri herself, painted on my first mug! I can't say I liked the way I looked when I attempted to do my own face a few weeks later though! Didn't look ANYTHING like the way it did when Jeff did my make-up.

Alisa Summers
I have always wanted to perform, or do something on stage, but as a boy I was just too shy. I originally decided to try club kid, and found myself a drag mother to help me achieve it. With time, I found myself not getting

anywhere, so I went to my current drag mother, Jocelyn Summers, and asked for help. The first time I got all dolled up and did a show felt amazing, and I knew that this what I wanted to be doing with my life.

Jeffrey Powell

It was a few months ago. I had been wanting to for a while and had befriended Crystle Chambers. So, one weekend I went and picked out an outfit and the next Thursday Crystle painted me and it was a blast!

Juwana Jackson

I was in college, around the age of 19. I at first did it as a bet. The first time was HORRIBLE, so I did it again the following semester. There, I was discovered by the President of the Gay Student Union, who invited me to a drag fundraising show for our Homecoming Float. I performed that evening, got a standing ovation, was invited to perform by the show director (The Lady Pearl) and the rest is history.

Crystal Belle

I think I was 19 and still living in the dorms of the college I attended. I loved doing it for Halloween and started doing it on open stage nights at a local bar. From then on, it's history. I now perform every night and feel oh so amazingly confident and sexy about myself!

Esme Russell

Well, I always felt female. To ask a transgender person this question is like asking a straight person when did you know you were straight , you don't know, you just are.

PurrZsa Kyttyn

I used to "borrow" my sister's clothes when she wasn't home and prance around in her heels while no one was home. I'd say I was in 4th grade.

Lacey Lynn Taylors

I have always been obsessed with all things female. Raised by my grandmother, I had the opportunity to see makeup being applied and hairpieces, jewelry. I started dressing up maybe around middle school age. I'm sure my grandmother wouldn't have liked knowing that on those snow days I was parading around the house in her prettiest dress.

Joey Brooks

I won a Talent Show at age 17. I loved the attention I was able to command from audience.

Glitz Glam
Halloween '96. I was in my early 20's, I think?~ it's a been awhile... I looked hideous. I used a wig I think my cat pissed in and I worked the shit out of a pink mini dress and white chunky platform heels! I was a HOT MESS!

Afeelya Bunz
Won't say I like dressing like a female, but enjoy entertaining as a female

Lady Liemont
I started as a Club Kid, I always knew i liked the transformation part of it. I am a shy guy as a boy, but as a performer I can be and do anything

Nairobi V. D'Viante
I was 21 and I just thought about how much fun I had being myself. jr. jeans , sparkly tops, and an odd pair of shoes, because it was all I could find that would fit my foot.

Patrice Knight
I was 19 going on 20, and I was in the Army in Germany. Some friends dared me to wear this hideous wig, but when I put it on they said I looked like Tina Turner without makeup. At that point I decided that I wanted to be a DRAG QUEEN.

Babette Schwartz
When I was 20, a friend and I saw a TRAGIC drag show in Oxnard, California. We decided we could do better, so we came back with a sister act that KILLED!

Raven Manniac
I did it for a contest called the Closet Ball. I did it because my partner at the time did drag and told me over and over that I didn't have what it took to carry it off. I made the top 10 my first time out... and the Monster was loose...

Twat Sisters
Sister Ima started earlier than Sister Ineeda. Sister Ineeda was in her late 20's when she first put on the makeup and dress for a talent contest at Rocky's Pub in Clearwater, Florida....from that moment on, I loved the attention!!!

Pussy Lahoot
In 1970, for Halloween, my mom dressed me up to go trick or treating in some of her things. My mom wasn't flashy, but surprisingly enough we were able to make me look like a 10 year old Joann Worley. I wore one of

her paisley blouses as a mini dress, her white fake fur winter coat, and her snow boots as go go's.... a little make up and an old shag wig bought for bad hair days and i was transformed.... everyone thought I was so pretty...and I remember thinking this is power...this is what i want!!!

Jade Daniels

Besides the one time in Drama Club, the cheerleading routine, and two HORRIBLE Halloween Costumes, I was never in full drag for the first time till I was 22...but even then I didn't "enjoy" it at first. I liked it, but I was extremely insecure and uncomfortable. It wasn't until the first time I performed on stage. It was such an amazing feeling of empowerment with the adrenaline flowing, the beat of the music, the big hair, fierce costume, and all the energy from the crowd screaming at you! It was that moment I knew I liked this!

Monique Michaels

I lived in Kentucky at the time. I was 16 and it was Halloween. My older sister had decided that I was going out in drag so we could go to a bar. I loved the power that looking like a vixen brought me, and the looks.

Jaeda Fuentes

I was 18 when I realized I liked to do drag. I liked to perform and entertain people and to be able to express myself through this character that I was creating. Amazing!

TotiYanah Diamond

I was 9. I would always wear a shirt on my head to make it into long hair. I always loved the fact of putting on makeup and smelling good with perfume. I would be in my mom's closet when she was working. Looking fabulous doll.

Leilani Masters

Age 31, two years ago.I wentto go to the store, spend money for female attire to put a look together for my character as I debut her on stage.

Amanda Lay-Boheme

I started wearing women's clothing when I was four years old. My sister, who is four years older than me, always played dress up with me and her clothes. I didn't mind though, I enjoyed it.

PurrZsa Kyttyn-Azrael

I remember dressing up in my sister's and mother's clothes for Halloween as far back as the age of 8. I used to borrow her "Brownies" and

"Pocahontas" outfits! Mother had this long black dress with colored polka dots that I would wear and be a pregnant clown!

Jenna Telia
I was 36 years old. I was a late bloomer, but everything has a season. I went to the local Salvation Army, located in an ignorant part of town in Pennsylvania. I marched right into the ladies dressing room, right in front of two old ladies in shock. I threw the dress on, and asked advice on how I looked in this skin tight nighty from my friend. I opened the door and the rumors started, it was so hot to be in a woman's outfit in such a religious thrift store. The only thing I hated was the smell of the place, B.O. and Shame. Otherwise, a spritz of perfume, and I was good to go. I always try on clothes in the ladies dressing rooms before I walk out with a purchase. Just have confidence, and some balls, and no one will say anything to you, and you may even open some minds. I was transformed into a Dumpster Diva with the help of my partner Glenn Storm, aka: Dmentia Divinyl. I always supported Glenn early on as a drag impersonator when he did shows at bars and club as "Eva LaDeva." I had an interest in being part of the glamour, however since I don't take dressing up as a women seriously and just for fun. I wanted to wait until I could find a way to do it for some laughs and entertainment, so low and behold, along came the character named "Jenna Telia", which was named after my mom, "Janet" and of course after my Junk in the front. Happy to say I only do drag when I feel like it. I don't answer to anyone, and I love the freedom to express myself as a clown as it should be!

Aime Jean
At age 26, when I went for the first time to USA. I was in shock of all the stuff I could get, and the opportunity to find my size shoes (women's 11), so I bought like an entire store. I started to dress up like a woman in 2002, at the age of 19, but i wished I could since i was 6, because there's no other thing that makes me more happy than wearing women's clothes. I live in Mexico, in a small town, where it was tough for me to be drag, but today I'm the queen of this land, and the people love me

Nostalgia Notanotherrerun Ronin
At 21, when I helped with a benefit at college. I had an emerging queen down the hall from me, and one of their friends suggested that my legs were so hairy that it wasn't worth shaving and to get four layers of pantyhose. I haven't shaved to this day. I grew up less than rich, where sometimes you got what you could get when it came to clothes and just ignored which side the buttons were placed on. I did drag once for a pediatric AIDS benefit at my college, but fell in love with it 6 months later, in 2003, when I realized my social anxiety was better when I couldn't be

recognized, and that as a big guy I couldn't change too much as a man, but lay it on as a woman.
 Dr. J.
Age 36. My first purchase was on eBay in the teenage boy sizes. My very first time putting on men's clothing, I was about 15 years. I came across my stepfather's jock strap while snooping in his dresser drawer for a cigarette. I remember putting it on and thinking hmmm...something is missing so I skipped my happy lil butt to the fridge and placed a cucumber in it. Back to the mirror, I went to check it out and that's when I said "that's what I'ma talking about!" ~ Stage name Dr J from Florida

Daisha Monet
I was 25 years old when I decided to go out and purchase women's attire. I went to a thrift store because a seasoned drag pro, aka my drag mother, told me that that was the place to go and find items to manipulate for the art of drag. It was a truly memorable moment in life that I will never ever forget. Everyone in the store was looking at me like OMG. But I was proud and comfortable with who I was. I was not bothered by what they had to say and think of me. The first time I decided to don women's clothing was for a HIV/AIDS benefit show that took place in Myrtle Beach, South Carolina. I must say that like many other of my cohorts, I was a little nervous at first. Soon, when I hit that stage, and the crowd started cheering me on, I felt more comfortable, as if I was home. I performed *I Need A Hero,* wearing of course a classic costume (the wonder woman look). I must say I looked sick, or awesome for those that don't understand drag lingo. I was 25 years of age at that time, and fresh out of the United States Navy (submarines). Today I'm 31 years of age, and performing at my best. Drag is my life, and if I had to do it all over again, I would choose drag every time.

Pimp Daddy (also performs as Lady Chabli)
I was 16 when I bought my first article of clothing. I love being the Pimp Daddy!!! I feel like that's the way I should look and feel all the time. My Frist title was Mister Glitz. I am Mr Buddys Coral and will be ending my two year reign in May 2013....I also have Sassy Chabli. She is awesome. Also i love the fact I do king and also drag and not as a woman in drag as a man. I was taught by an amazing queen Dion Martel Wright.

Stefon Royce Iman
I started at age 14. My mother would say you are not a boy. I thought clearly otherwise, I was. I have a twin brother. I always went in his room and took his clothes and wore them.

Alexis Mateo, King Aramis, and Yara Sofia
Photo By: Danielle Multer

Melissa Mason, Joey Brooks,
Robyn DeMornay, and Summer Alexander
Photo By: Junstin Duncan

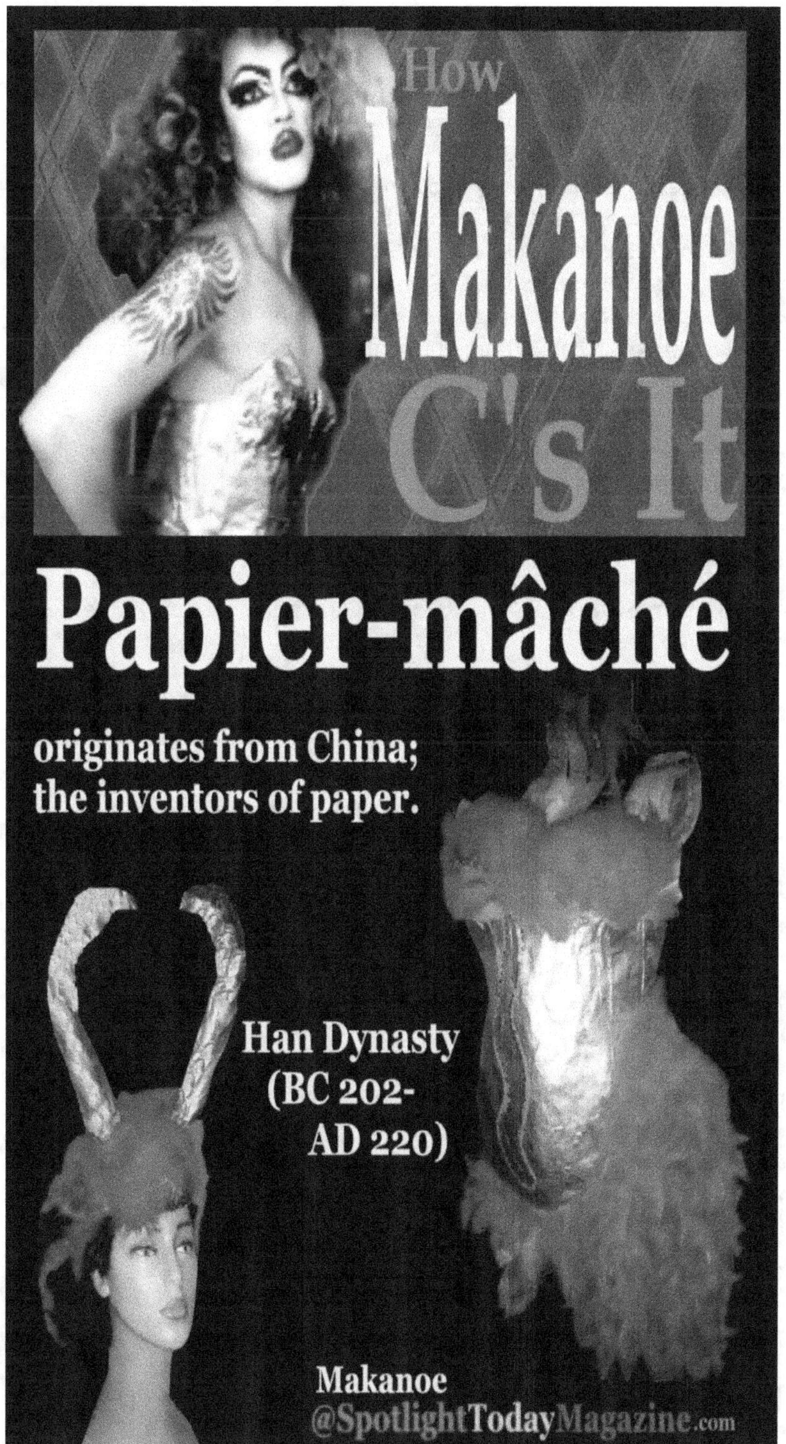
How
Makanoe
C's It
Papier-mâché
originates from China;
the inventors of paper.
Han Dynasty
(BC 202-
AD 220)
Makanoe
@SpotlightTodayMagazine.com

Love & Beauty to You,

This is your Royal Highness of the Leo monarchs.

Yes, I am a Leo, and I am beautiful!

In this issue of SPOTLIGHT TODAY Magazine, I will write about making accessories using easy and simple methods. It is sloppy, but well worth the time and mess once you realize your final art piece.

This takes me back to when I was a kid sporting a forest green matching polyester pant suit with a bowl haircut that went with the times. Do not judge me, do not judge me! Mrs. Clothier was my teacher when I was five years old. I can still smell her mixture of hairspray and Bengay.

She taught us how to make papier-mâché piggy banks.

Did any of you make these pigs?

I believe it is standard kindergarten craft. I remember loving creating my piggy. It was all kinds of wrong, but I loved that pig!

I believe it started my artistic career and the subject of this issue's column. You can tell by the prior pages inset photographs, my interpretation of a Lady Gaga devil outfit with horns. You can craft anything from a simple arm band, or let your creativity flow to create anything you desire.

These simple instructions will get you started.

1. This is the paste I normally use, because it's stronger than boiled paste, and you can complete a project with only a few layers of paper.
2. To create the paste, pour white flour in a bowl, and add water gradually until you have a consistency that will work well. (Use a small kitchen mixer to avoid lumps). It is up to you to determine its thickness. Experiment with thick pastes that resemble hotcake batter or thin pastes that are runny and watery. You get to decide which ones you prefer. Keep in mind that it is the flour, and not the water, that gives strength to your papier-mâché creation.
3. Remember each layer of paste and paper added to your project must dry completely to keep it from developing mold. Speaking of mold, why not use wallpaper pastes containing fungicides? There are two reasons why I choose to use white flour pastes, instead of ingredients that prevent mold. White flour is ridiculously cheap when compared to any other type of art supply. I hate the idea of dipping my hands in something that contains poison, often the ingredient in products that prevent mold. I put enough poison in my body. Remember, molds cannot grow without water.
4. Take every effort to dry out your projects completely. The main trick is to make sure the sculpture is completely dry, it is as simple as that. Dry all the way through – if any dampness is left inside when you apply paint or

other finish, the sculpture will eventually rot from the inside out – a truly disappointing development, I assure you.

5. It is good to save your old newspaper ads. Sometimes I will go pick up some of those free newspapers (if I am feeling ghetto), but mostly I use nice 11x14 white paper. It is more expensive, but it tends to be easy to shape, plus it's white offering it more versatility. Tear the paper into strips or chunks, whichever is your preference. You will want to cover the the table and floor with newspaper or plastic cover. Paper-mâché is messy.

6. Borrow or use your "dress form." because to make the unique pieces you will need one. Invest in a used or new. Whatever, it is worth it. If you have a friend that is stupid enough to stand there, you can paste this on them and wait for it to dry. My friends do not love me that much.

7. Cover the dress form in plastic to prevent ruining it, I will just design with tape how I want it to look on the dress form first, then I start putting layers. Dip your paper in paste and add layer after layer, and do not be lazy, put a full layer on one at a time, so it is consistent and it is thick. A good piece will take patience and eight layers.

8. You can make a half corset, a full one covering the hip area, or even a bra type piece. When done layering, let it dry for a few days. If you have sun, stick it outside to dry faster. After it is dry, take a blade out of your hair, or any retractable knife. Careful cut the back of the piece without slicing your dress form or your friend. Pry it apart. It will most likely be moist inside - get your mind out of the gutter!

9. Let it sit a day or two. If you have a heater, put it near the heater. Use heavy duty scissors to trim the fat off to make it nice and pretty.

10. Once you are done trimming the edges, use an ice pick, or if you're butch like me, use a drill to drill a few holes on each side of the back. Tie string through the holes. Be sure and use heavy duty string, not yarn. Use common sense.

11. To become creative, I use metallic spray paint. Now don't freakin' inhale the stuff. It will kill your brain cells, and if you're like me you cannot afford to lose what you got. The spray will make it look like metal.

12. Add some gems or feathers, so can you sport your new creation in your next show, and everyone will be drooling over your new costume.

      If they ask you were you got it, say you made it, because you did, and refer them to SPOTLIGHT TODAY Magazine 's to get their own tips from Makanoe. I don't have much sense, 'cause I am pretty, but I got some ideas that work most of the time.

      Papier-mâché is cheap and easy, and you don't have to be a genius to be creative. If you want to make earrings or bangle bracelets, you can use a soda can to do your layers. For earrings lay your layers on a cookie sheet and use cookie cutters to make shapes. I can go on and on, but they only give a so many words, so there you go.

Papier-mâché is not just for kindergarten piggy banks anymore, and that is how Makanoe sees it!

Londenn D. Raine, MiMi Welch, Whitney, & Chanel LaMasters
Photo Credit: Timothy Joyner

Karambas Night Club – Eva LaDeva, Fac Ade, Katrina Fatale,
Patricia Mason, Savannah Stevens
Photo By: Vincent J. Wiercinski

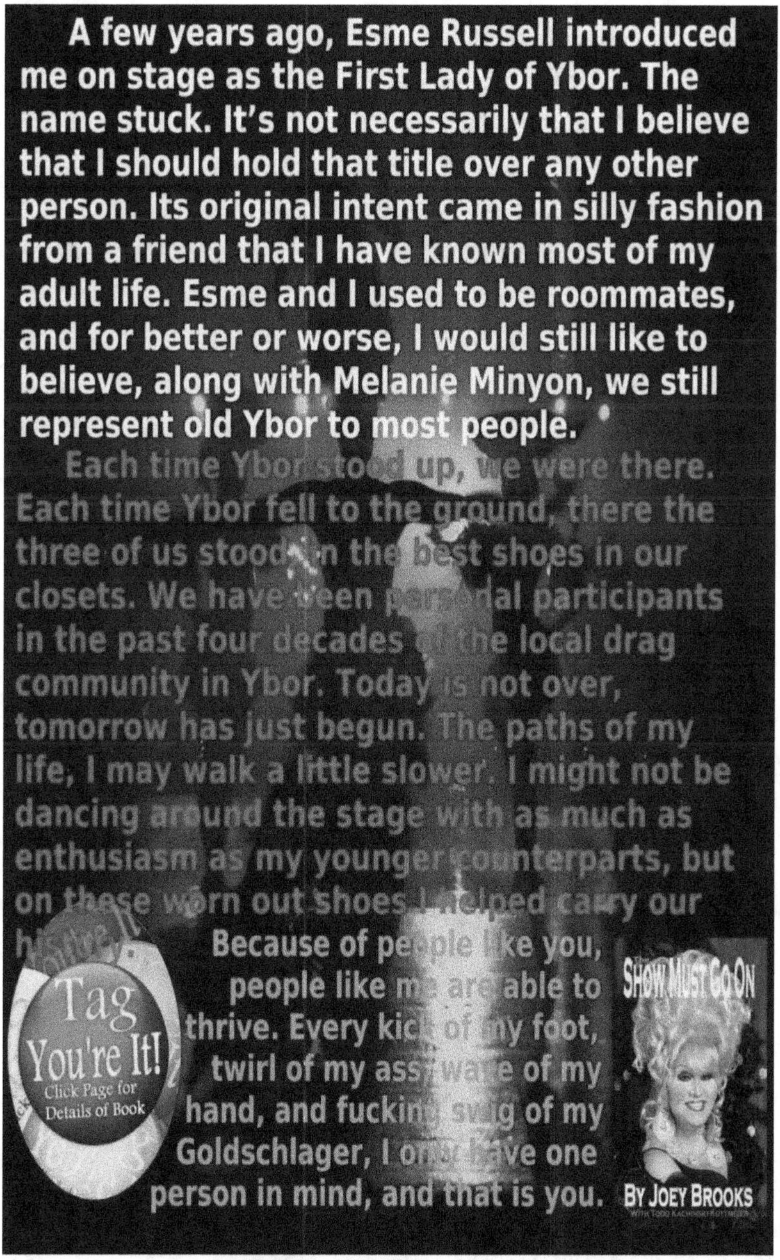
A few years ago, Esme Russell introduced me on stage as the First Lady of Ybor. The name stuck. It's not necessarily that I believe that I should hold that title over any other person. Its original intent came in silly fashion from a friend that I have known most of my adult life. Esme and I used to be roommates, and for better or worse, I would still like to believe, along with Melanie Minyon, we still represent old Ybor to most people.
Each time Ybor stood up, we were there. Each time Ybor fell to the ground, there the three of us stood in the best shoes in our closets. We have been personal participants in the past four decades of the local drag community in Ybor. Today is not over, tomorrow has just begun. The paths of my life, I may walk a little slower. I might not be dancing around the stage with as much as enthusiasm as my younger counterparts, but on these worn out shoes I helped carry our history.
Because of people like you, people like me are able to thrive. Every kick of my foot, twirl of my ass, wave of my hand, and fucking swig of my Goldschlager, I only have one person in mind, and that is you.
Tag You're It!
Click Page for Details of Book
Show Must Go On
By Joey Brooks

Joey Brooks, The Show Must Go On
Available through DRAG411.com

This is for the spouses of illusion. You may not know us, as we are the ones sitting quietly while our spouses show people "how it's done."

ThomasDeVoyd
@SpotlightTodayMagazine.com

"The audience does get a piece of them,
but we get to take them home"

Sometimes it's nice to sit quietly back unobserved. You are in a sense, the Jane Goodall of the illusion scene. It gives you the opportunity to gauge the crowd's reaction. Our spouses listen to us because there is no ulterior motive. We aren't sharing our knowledge to cut them down or destroy their self-esteem. We do it out of love. Most of the crowd wouldn't notice, because spouses wait until no one is around to give our opinions. Well, depending on the night and the state of the illusionist that we love, we may wait until the next day.

As a spouse, you learn to do things that you never thought you would. I have learned to put wigs together and stone costumes. I also buy many of the outfits and jewelry because I have a decent eye. If my spouse doesn't like it, there is always someone who will. I think I would call that, "my spotlight". I think we all find our spotlight, because we know there will be times we sit in the bar only to play games on our phones; it is also part of what we do. We don't feel neglected. We know that our counterparts are doing their job, and do not have a vendetta against us. They aren't trying to make us feel badly.

You meet many people being a spouse including other illusionists, their spouses (which is nice because then you have someone to sit with), and bartenders. It is great getting to know people. The spouse has to be both a social butterfly and a wall flower. We are there for our spouses.

You also become the MacGyver of the dressing room. You keep a stock of essentials including safety pins, clips, combs, hose, tape, glue, and always a jewelry repair kit. This isn't only for our spouse, but if someone needs something, we are there for them too. We also may be our spouse's or anyone of needs dresser. You learn to get good at handling situations and it becomes part of who we are. Some spouses are better than others, but I have to say I have never heard a spouse say no to someone asking for help getting dressed. This is also how we share in the performance.

I think one of the important things I do, is take pictures. I take hundreds of pictures. I have to say I'm grateful for digital cameras. I would have had to file bankruptcy long ago trying to buy film. I'll take pictures of everyone, which means learning to take better photographs. I have to admit this is the reason I accumulate hundreds of pictures.

Out of the group, I am trying to get ten pictures that will make everyone happy. I learned long ago to bring spare batteries in my MacGyver bag. When you are trying to remove old batteries and put in new batteries in the dark, with music blaring, and expectations for pictures running high, you feel a bit like the paparazzi. I know that might seem selfish, but it's another task I love about being a spouse.

The biggest part being a spouse of an illusionist is... just being there. The entertainers run around talking to everyone and the spouse may feel ignored but later they come up to you, give you a kiss and tell you they love you. Those are the simple moments that make everything worthwhile. It makes carrying the bags, taking the pictures, and making sure they didn't forget anything worth it.

The audience does get a piece of them, but we get to take them home. Spouses, we are united doing what we do, and loving who we do it for. So next time you are in the bar and see people sitting on the sidelines with a camera, ten purses, while monitoring drinks, just remember it is probably a spouse of one of the performers.

Spouses of illusionists: though we might be a little jealous of who they are talking to, but in the end it is us they want to take home.

Did you know 100% of the gross advertising sales are donated to benefit Hunger America, is donated by you directly to MCC TAMPA, so you receive a 100% tax deduction? At no point does a single person earn a single penny creating this project. Every word shared, every hour donated, every soul we touch... comes from the hope of all of us creating a better path to walk together.

San Francisco Pride
Photo By: Vincent J. Wiercinski

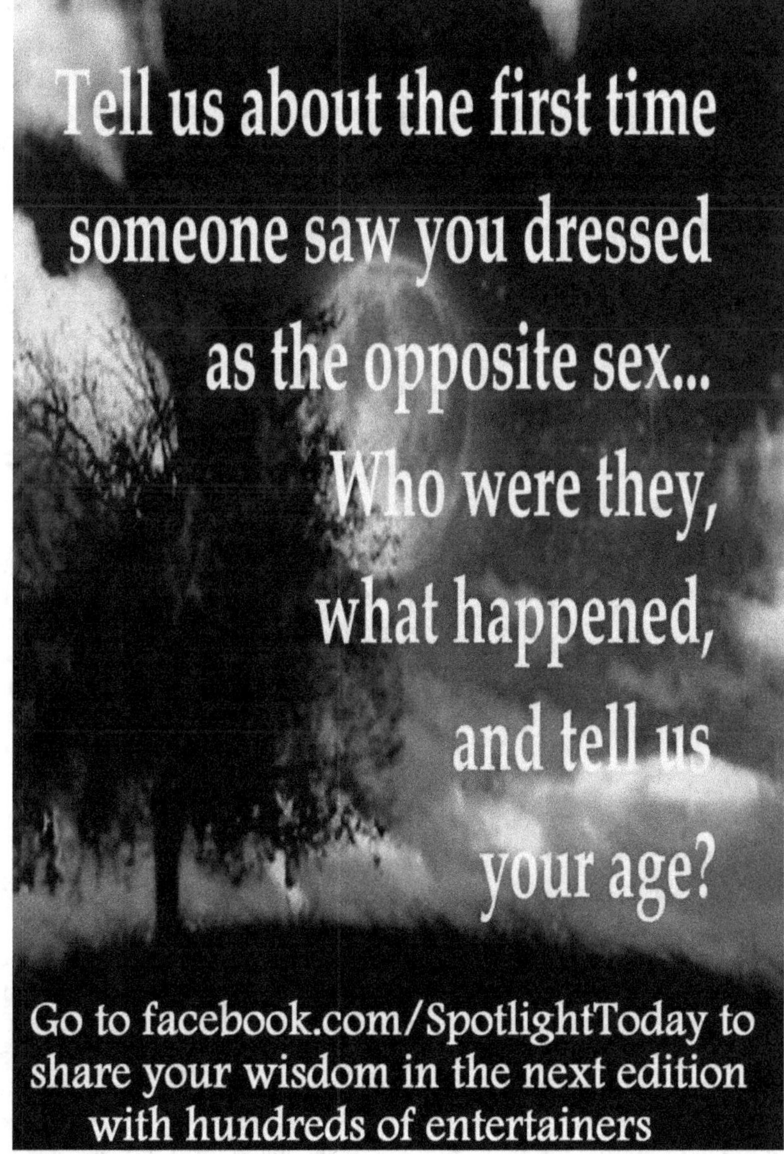

Esme Russell
Well, that would be the queen who actually put me in drag. Her name was Chena Black. She was beautiful, and I was 15 years old.

PurrZsa Kyttyn
18. The first time I ever went to a gay bar. I went in my mom's old dress (turned out to be a dated wedding gown), and I was alone. I sat on the

front row to watch the show. I was nervous and excited. I wanted to watch a drag show. Turns out... there were strippers there. Then one of them puts his thong clad crotch in my face and I turned my head because I was shy back then. Then show director calls out on the mic "girl, don't sit on the front row if you're not going to look"...I was so mortified I got up and ran out!

Lacey Lynn Taylors
The first time anyone saw me dressed in drag was at the Beaux Arts Ball in Lexington, KY. I was 20 years old, and I looked a mess as far as drag goes, but I didn't know that then. My friends didn't recognize me and I had all the straight guys fooled!

Joey Brooks
The talent show was the first time I had put on a dress.

Aime Jean
May 22 -2002. I was impersonating Thalia, wich is one of my favorite artists, and who serves me as inspiration. I was 19, and my friends and I decided to make a show in a bar near my town in Mexico. We made a show (very very poor), but I had lots of fun and since that show I'm still on the road

Sybil Storm
Robin Knight (may she rest) and I was amazed.

Jenna Telia
I was 36 years old. The first time I dressed up as my campy alter ego named, "Jenna Telia" in public, it was at a local Gay Campground in Pennsylvania called "Hillside Campground". Yup, that's right, an outdoor bathhouse with campers, tents and outhouses. I was having difficulty walking the rocky slopes and terrain in heels for my very first time. Once I got the hang of it, I sashayed my way around like a June Bug. Since it was September 2009, it got a bit chilly and the bugs tried to eat me through my girdle. I just never saw so many shocked faces when my friends, who never saw me in drag, told me how good I actually pulled it off. It was a night I will never forget, and there are pictures to prove it.

PurrZsa Kyttyn-Azrael
I was a pregnant clown for my school Halloween costume party in 7th grade! I won that year!

Horchata
21, in front of some roommates and some people at a bar. They were surprised because they didn't know. It was Halloween, and it was a given. It wasn't until a while later on when I started going out in drag.

Michael Wilson
I was 18 and Jamie Summers (from NC) said, "if I had eyelashes like that I wouldn't own a pair of false ones."

Dr. J.
I was 35 when I decided to give the drag king a try. One night a friend and I decided to practice at my house. I wanted to try performing as Tom Cruise did in the movie Risky Business where he slid across the floor in socks and underwear and an open button down shirt. Only my undies had a very large sock stuffed in 'em. That was the first time my daughter, then 10 years old, saw me. She fell over laughing and yelling "scarred for life"

Naomi Wynters
I was about 19. It was with some of my friends. We were sitting around. They were drag queens. They tried to get me into drag, and I wasn't feeling it. They finally talked me into doing so. The next time my official drag presence, was during turnabout for a club I was working at. It went from there and i slowly began to fall in love

Deva DaVyne
At 17, I decided to go out with my friend on a night that she had a house party, and i dressed up. I was a mess back then, but people really loved it, and i had a lot of people tell me that i was brave for dressing and stepping out the house.

Stephen Brooks
It was Halloween. I was WRONG at every level, but my friends said I was beautiful!! Looking back at pics, BOY were they good friends!!

Nostalgia Notanotherrerun Ronin
I was 21, it was Halloween, and I was a manager at a fast food chain. I changed in the bathroom after work, but had to go back behind the counter and assist the relief manager. All my employees loved it, but a guy at the window called me a *** and I had to run to stop an employee from chasing them.

Felina Cashmere
Aside from my mother dressing me in my sister's clothes when we were younger, when I actually did it in the name of "drag," everyone thought I

was a girl. Even my friends were amazed to see the outcome of being painted. Straight guys would hit on me, and one thought I was someone's mother.

Kier
Showed the movie to our class, a lot of guys said who's the hot goth chick

Amanda Love
My boyfriend came home to find me wearing a leopard print dress and heels and hose, no wig or makeup. He damn near passed out. We still laugh about it. That evening, my drag mothers came over, and well that was the beginning of the end. .

Trixie Scott
January 3rd 2008. It was the first time someone dressed me up, put makeup on my face, and said you're a drag queen. To see everyone's reaction, and the compliments I was getting, was great. It was the start to one amazing adventure

Maxine Padlock
Before I really did drag, a couple of years before I became Maxi PAD, I was Cher Candy and dressed up all out fishy and went to my mother's house. I knocked and started walking in past her and she was like can I help you? I said Ma? And she was like OMG !! She actually thought I was one of her boyfriend's hoochie mamas . That was a good one. And, she wanted to wear my hair.

Papi Chulo
The first time someone saw me dressed like the opposite sex was at a Halloween party a few years back. I dressed like a biker dude from head to toe. Friends were shocked at how good I looked, and how believable I was. They were green with envy!! Papi Chulo struck again!!!

Mike Asterman
It was the night of the first show at the club, and all the people I knew did not believe it

Butt Wiser
I was 12 and my friends laughed at me. It hurt, but my dream was to be a "Carol Burnett" style character.

Amanda Bone
I was 18 and I'm pretty sure it was my mom and my friend Damien. My mom said I don't get it, you're a big ole boy, you look like a football player

in girl's clothes. My friend just cosigned all my crazy, so he was like you look fishy bitch. My mom said, "dog fish," lmao

Patrice Knight
I finally frocked it up in front of my best friend when we were 21 and he didn't even recognize me. I sat at the bar next to him for about 10 minutes before I broke the ice with, "Girl, you gonna sit there all night and not say hello?" He was so shocked he almost fell off the barstool.

Misty Eyes
I was nine.... I got caught by everyone... My mother, my grandmother... my neighbors. I was a secret obsession, but I guess the whole town knew and there was a HUGE intervention. They told me I was a boy, etc., and boys don't wear dresses

Diamond Dunhill
It would have to be the patrons of The FRITZ Gay Sports Bar in Boston, MA. Halloween Night 1998. "19" and we were the AZN Invasion, Yeast Inspection Gurlz! Winning Best Group that night! We were a hit with the boyz!

Miss Gigi
Same as the first question, it was at work, and they all fell out. I actually fooled our General manager and assistant manager. They thought I was a new employee. After that I was taken all over work and everyone was jealous because I had better legs then most of the women. One girl had me walk with her. Not knowing, she walked me by a gay guy who loved drag or cd men, and he was locked on me the whole time. She laughed the whole time, and after she told me what she did......

Makanoe
The first time someone saw me as a girl, I was 17 years old. It was my friend who was straight as a doornail. His name was James, (He had the best hairy legs ever, 19 years old and I had the biggest crush on him. Well he asked me to this Halloween party. He went as George Washington and so I went as Martha. He didn't expect me to look that good as a girl. Let's just say, he had a few drinks on purpose, and I did my wifely duties with no one speaking of it the next day. He joined the Navy that next summer and I never heard from him again except a picture that he sent me in his navy uniform after boot-camp. That was it. My sister still has it.

Stefon Royce Iman
The first time someone saw me dressed up as a man I was like 28. It was my cab driver. I jumped into the car not realizing I still had facial hair on.

He had the biggest crush on me as a female. He said wait Toni that is you. I said yes, drive me home, and don't tell anyone you saw me like this.

Diedra Windsor Walker
It would be Halloween and my favorite response was from Blake Hardcastle, my supervisor. He saw me walk into the club on Halloween and said, "GOOD LORD....YOU LOOK LIKE A CROSS BETWEEN JULIA SUGARBAKER & MADEA, QUEEN!" I was 30 yrs. old and I remember wearing heels that killed me. I was with a fraternity brother, who soon assumed the identity Bethany Boudreaux. At the time, my name was Ima Giho.

Kiki LaFlare Santangilo
I went out with some friends to P.F. Changs dressed as a woman, and they loved it! It started out with just myself and one friend, but by the weekend we had about 6 girls that wanted to go with us! Our waiter was extremely handsome and he kept calling us "ladies" and "ma'am"...they were dying from laughter! Our server probably thought we were crazy, because he didn't realize I was a man. It was very entertaining.

Adrian Leigh
I was 16 and my then GIRL friend dressed me for Halloween. I was a girl, and she was a guy.

Anastasia Fallon
Actually, I have a fun story about the first time my Dad saw me dressed. It was after I'd been living with my Mom, and working at City Limits, in Brandon, FL (My very first home bar!). I got all dressed up, and walked out, luggage in tow, and looked over at my Dad on the couch. My Mom could barely contain herself, she was used to the sight by now, he was not. All he really said was a joke, common encouragement in my family. "Hope you don't get pulled over." Without missing a beat, I looked over, "Well Dad, I think it is the cop that has to worry about that, hope I don't confuse him too much."

Champagne T. Bordeaux
19, my drag-mom, she was the one whom i made the bet with. I was bitter, then bout 120 folks 20 min later. Talk about getting thrown to the wolves.. They ate me up too. The club was "the grotto" in Columbus Ohio.

Barbra Herr
It was at a club...many people.

Mis Sadistic
The first time was in a Fourth of July Parade in the town I grew up in. I was picked with some of the other kids I went to school with to be in the Parade. I was Betsy Ross. No one could talk me out of it either. I went down the main street in our town on a float. I was about age seven. Funny thing was nobody knew it was me at first, I looked so much like a real girl. I remember getting called all kinds of mean names afterwards, and my mother got a a lot of flak over letting me do it, from friends and family.

Cathy Craig
My sisters, they said I was prettier than them. I still am.

Lady Tajma Hall
After being dressed as a girl all of my childhood by my mother, I spent my life thinking I was born as a girl! I was 20 when I decided I would go all out and be a girl in drag! I did a benefit show for the late Ashley Reynolds in Fayetteville, NC and received so many compliments. Terri Vanessa Coleman saw me and took me under her wings. It was the beginning of a career that started some years later.

Jocelyn Summers
First time I went out was after a break up with someone in the drag scene. I went to the Miss Orlando Pageant in'98 and everyone's jaw dropped, the Jason they knew was replaced by a lady.

Jade Shanell
I was 33 years old and getting ready for work for the Halloween party. I was walking into work, and a coworker friend of mine walked past me and then turned around and said my name and I turned around and said no way is that you. She just lit up and looked me all over and said damn girl you look fine, I'm jealous that you look better than me and God made what I got. I was thinking wow, snap snap for me baby.

Kori Stevens
It wasn't such a big deal.....I was never seen as a girl until I "DID IT UP" for Halloween at 26 years of age.

Brianna Lee
Me as a girl? I was not in a dress, but I was 12 and dressed up for Halloween as *Laverne De Fazio* of Laverne and Shirley. Yes, with the big L on the chest. My neighbor was the first to see me and thought I was an identical twin to my boy self.

Makayla Rose Devine
My mother, and she didn't know what to say !

Vivika D'Angelo
Age 22, my mom. She looked at me and said, "is it my fault that you are dressing up? You look adorable you are a guy, remember that."

Toni DaVyne
My 16th birthday! I had decided that I wanted to be a princess and got all decked out as a girl with help from my sister.

Michelle Tatum
The first person to see me in my drag persona were my best friends. They had been doing drag for years and they were older . That's how I got into the bars so young.

Conundrum
First off, anytime a Boy/Man dresses as a Girl/Woman it always directs a lot of attention towards that person. Unfortunately, I don't remember when or who saw me the first time, but I do remember trying on makeup one day and someone rang my door bell. I tried to wash it off so fast and answer the door that I didn't completely remove the makeup. I remember the question "are you wearing Make-up?" Needless to say I was a little embarrassed that I was caught!

Naomi D-Lish
My own father didn't recognize me. First night I was ever out and my parents showed their support. Mom came first and dad later. Dad didn't know who the tall chick on his shoulders was. hahaha

Katrina Starr
My sister painted my face and put a bra and my mother's clothes on me. We laughed so hard, we cried

Pimp Daddy (also performs as Sassy Chabli)
My wifey, and she thought I was sexy. Friends didn't know me.

Wendy G Kennedy
My wife. She was a bit freaked out. She`s straight as an arrow.

Beverly LaSalle
The first time anyone saw me in drag, I was 17 years old, living in Key West. I painted up, and went out to the local bars. My friends couldn't believe it

was me! I had the best time, and was encouraged to start performing. That night was also the night I received my first invitation to do a guest spot, and my career was born!!!

Jade Jolie
My first roommate heard me clucking in my shoes on the tile. Luckily, they were completely supportive and even pushed me to continue further.

Daisha Monet
My sister was the first to see me in full drag. I was at her house getting my costume together for the benefit show. She was thrilled to see the transformation. I'm 31 years of age and love the drag queen life.

Jami Micheals
I was 19 and I went out after my now ex boyfriend painted me and we went to Warehouse 29 in Greensboro. The patrons were very nice and told me I was pretty

Dmentia Divinyl
age 12, my Mom She caught me wearing her heels and dancing around in the living room to music. At first, she laughed and then scolded me for going through her belongings, Can you blame her...?

Geraldine Queencabaret
I had a plan to do it for the first time in public. I wanted to test myself if I'd be strong enough to do it in public, so I had talked to my sister and she gave me her little black dress, a blue scarf (she had no wig) an eyeliner and some little sheer make up she had (which covered nothing at all). I had to assist a barbeque in a rooftop at night where close friends of mine had invited me. Without them knowing, one moment after dinner I disappeared and showed up 20 minutes later dressed up. I remember going upstairs to the rooftop where they were, and that little last step I had to take for them to see me was the most difficult step in my life. I was scared, shaking, happy, afraid, horrified, and exited at the same time. I wanted to run away, but at the same time, I wanted to do it so badly. I finally took the chance and pushed myself up that step, and they all were shocked. They wouldn't say a word, so I told them, " Hi guys...this is me...the real me...I am not expecting you to tell me how good I look, I didn't even shave my legs, and I am barefoot (I had no shoes/heels). I am not looking to look pretty. I am expecting you to accept me the way I am. You can ask me the questions I have been asking and answering to myself for the past 24 years, because I don't wanna hide and cry no more. This is me, the same person you know, and I need to talk about this, so don't be afraid and ask me whatever comes to your mind." After that, I went and

sat on the table and they asked me 1000 questions and more. I had never felt so happy and pure in my whole life....and with my hairy legs , my eyeliner ,my sheer make up that covered nothing and barefoot I had never felt so pretty...because I was accepted...and that can make all of us feel BEAUTIFUL.

Alisa Summers
For me, the first time anyone saw me in drag was when I entered a local talent contest. I was 19 years old at the time. I invited all of my friends, and they all came out to show support. No one could believe that it was me. Their reactions were pretty hilarious.

Angela Dodd
At Keri Nichols home, it wasn't a planned painting, it just sort of happened. Big Mamma B put a brown flipped bob wig on my head. I clutched a couch pillow to show above my neck so we could take some pictures of all my beauty! Angie (my namesake) was there and we all laughed and joked. It was very fun. It was a very life changing moment and I thank both of them for helping me that day! Oops, I was 21!

Jeffrey Powell
A few people who knew me didn't recognize me at first and others' jaws just dropped, probably only because of the element of surprise. I was 21.

Demonica da Bomb
I was 18. Lots of people at JR's Night Club. The Show Director, Amber Michaels, came up and told me I looked just like Nany Newton - who went on to be Ms. US of A at Large in '92.

Juwana Jackson
My best friend from high school saw me and said "FIERCE!" Well, of course we both were gay and came out to each other at the same time! We were both 19.

Crystal Belle
They were actually pleasantly surprised because they were impressed that I could actually look like a woman. It was incredibly nerve racking and I was just hoping I wouldn't fall over and die from the excitement. It was a great night over all, and back then we could still get into the bar when we were 19. I am now glad that all of my friends got to see me when we were young and could do all kinds of crazy things. They still come see me regularly but it was amazing when I first started and so exciting. It still gets me a little when I put on my lashes!

Glitz Glam
That was on Halloween night, I was 21years old. The entire club watched my train wreck come through!

Afeelya Bunz
People in Phoenix, it was in a bar.

Lady Liemont
My best Friend. He couldn't believe it. We went out and strutted our stuff. Had a blast

Patrice Knight
I was 20 when my Army friend Amy Fuller said that she wanted to help me do drag. She loaned me one of her gowns and did my makeup and hair. I went to a Fashion Party and many of the people in the club could not believe it was me.

Raven Manniac
MY ex - the guy who put me in drag. He said I looked like Bette Davis. I don't know if that was good or bad...

Pussy Lahoot
As a preteen, I was always mistaken for a girl. It was 1972, and I had typical long boy hair bleached from the summer sun. I was thin and was tan. I looked like a girl. I rode my bike up to the corner store one night and this 24 year old guy started talking to me, he thought i was a girl. We ended up pulling around the corner in his truck, and I masturbated him. I didn't even know what I was doing really. He showed me what to do, and when he "came" I didn't know what it was. He said, "that's what makes babies.". He kissed me and asked me to meet him the next night, and I did. He never touched me. I sometimes wonder if he knew I was a boy...who cares, I was hooked!

Rickie Lee
I am now 60...And you expect me to remember this HOW???

Jade Daniels
It was Sept. 3, 2000 and I was 22. My Drag Mother, Heather Daniels, put me in full drag from head to toe for the first time. We were at the Legendary Backstreet here in Atlanta, and it was Labor Day Weekend. It was kind of a "dress rehearsal", because I was going to be performing for the first time that Wed. night. So I was with my best friend Shane, and told him he could not tell anyone who I was! We hung out in the bar and our friends would come up to us and talk and hang out, and they would all ask,

"where is James?" Shane would gesture his head towards me without saying anything, and everyone FREAKED out! They thought I was a real girl and could not believe it was me. We stopped and talked to some other friends, and after we walked away one of them says, "Who was that girl with Shane?" He then chased us down because he had to see for himself, because he didn't believe it either!

Felina Cashmere and the trio of Greg and Victor form Rainbow411.com joining Kori Stevens

TotiYanah Diamond
It was Halloween, I was 14 yrs old. I was a bride. It was my family and a boy named Jason, who I liked. He pretended to be my husband that night. We even had fun after trick or treating was over.

Vegas Platinum
I went to a family friend's Halloween party! THEY WERE SO SURPRISED!

Jaeda Fuentes
It was Halloween. I was 18 and it was one of the most amazingly fun Halloweens Ever!

Flex Night Club
Raleigh, NC

CeCe Douglas-Ross, Valarie Rockwell,
Miss Trixie

Photo By: Vincent J. Wiercinski

Cosmic Queen by Camille Sands

The
Cameltoe
Monologues
CleanStorm
@SpotlightTodayMagazine.com

Bonjour Mon Homo-sapiens!

It is me, the guy who put the "Mad" in "Madam", Glenn Storm.

For all of you who do not have a clue of who I am, let me, intro-douche myself, my drag persona names are: "Eva LaDeva" and "Dmentia Divinyl". I was unable to pick which name to come out of the closet to write this column for SPOTLIGHT TODAY Magazine. I decided to write is as my male-self and give them both some kudos when available, using twenty years of female illusions and observations.

My column is about, "How to get away with bearing your soul and your cameltoe in order to aroused audience to demand seeing you as a performer. I have gathered a chock-full of personal stories, experiences, and tips on how to be a "Dumpster Diva" on a budget, but still see your name in lights on the leader boards around the globe.

What is a "Dumpster Diva" you ask?

I follow in the footsteps of those who have come before me such as; Divine, Star Booty, Hedda Lettuce, Lady Bunny and a gaggle of other gay gooses in feathers. A true "Dumpster Diva" makes tacky seem trendy. Start a fad by wearing something that looks like you literally found it in the trash and wear it with pride.

Concentrate more about what you are trying to say with your make-up and style, than trying just to look presentable. In order to shine, one has to look behind the curtain to see the little child running the projector. Once you do this, you can play dress up and come across as a fierce force. You can look incredible no matter the price of your makeup supplies, or gaudy and grotesque of a gown that you wear.

The squeaky wheel gets oiled or can be replaced. Hopefully after reading my tidbits in each issue in this illustrious magazine, you will soon be on your way to slumming to stardom. I must mention that "Monster Drag" can be fun, but it also can scare people in the process, just like any good haunted house, you should look inviting, but not too comfortable for people to stare.

I am speaking to all the drag queens and kings portraying themselves as clowns or impersonators for the sake of lively entertainment. My column is about running away to join a circus of freaks, and become a club kid with originality and flair. I challenge you to dare to take risks in experimental theatrics. Do not be afraid to take questionable approaches to dressing to parody or compliment a celebrity or persona created in your head.

Give your identity its own unique voice to play off a certain type of characteristic of behavior. The more you can commit to the character, the more money you will be able to cash in for doing live shows, theater, film and both photo shoots for commercials and advertising.

Pretend that your face is a coloring book, and the make-up you select is like a box of crayons. Unless you meant to color outside the lines, do not because it will look sloppy. Apply your face products and finger paints by hand. Getting used to using professional tools of the trade may prevent you from coming across as playful and unique. Unless you are into "paint by number" with watercolors, I would scrap the brush sets.

Try breaking the rules in the beginning to make your audience beg for more if you. The easier you make your face, the harder it is to mess up your face. Being consistent for your paparazzi, so be sure you know who you are before you try to be someone else.

When I put on my Dmentia Divinyl face, I make sure the eyebrows are rounded and high like "Bozo the Clown." The eye shadow is bold colors, streaking up the sides of my temples like flames from hell. I create contrast to give the illusion that my persona may be a little touched, or on too many medications to hold her hand perfectly steady to apply her own makeup. This will make people feel comfortable that they do not have to judge you for a beauty contestant, since all is lost in translation.

My makeup serves as a fright factor warning others that I may be a serial killer on a rampage. Just like a "Beware of Dog" sign, it can act as a bodyguard in some creepy dives and dumps where you are booked in bad areas of town. Who wants to mug someone looking jumped already, or may turn the blade on the villain?

The trick with doing "Dumpster Drag" is to being prepared to be crass when you need rude comments. Sometimes, when "Dmentia Divinyl" poses for a mug shot with a crowd of drunken losers, she may decide to blurt out before the flash bulb goes off, how she just farted. She smiles, laughs, or sometimes frowns to ensure the picture is worth sharing with their friends. Who wants to see a pretty picture of a drag queen huddled with their admirers? Where's the story behind the shot?

This column is preparing you to terrorize the public with drag. Drag terrorists are famous for being crude in public places. Anyone can see drag imitating life in the form of art. Some famous people who understood this perspective include Grace Jones, Elvira Mistress of the Dark, Pee Wee Herman, David Bowie, and Lady Gaga. These rebels without a cause, made being a freak fabulous and sought after. The person you portray in drag is someone normally not seen in public during the daytime, but also has a sign on them stating, "I am Free to Express Myself, and you can't do a thing about it".

Controversy pisses off people. They love an underdog, someone making them feel safe in a world where everyone is constantly judged by their cover. Be proud to buy from a second hand thrift store and seen at a Goodwill clothing and shoes. Wash and disinfect items you purchase second hand. I learned the hard way when I bought a used bathing suit. The previous owner had a case of crabs, so they donated them along with the garment. Luckily, I was not infected, but someone who tried the suit on for me had to run to the local pharmacy for some head lice gelatin and a comb set.

It pays to have an assistant to model your runway road kill fashions before you dare to bear it yourself. Used wigs can have head lice, so treat them with bleaches and strong detergents prior to use. Your character should look like the type of person whom you would get an infestation from if you stood next to them long enough, but it should be an illusion.

You do not need negative press early on in your career of making trashy classy and wanting to get paid for it. Once you get good at spotting bargain basement discounted things to wear, you can start collecting of accessories. Invest in a quality hot glue gun with plenty of glue sticks. Safety pins tend to open during your number on stage and become painful, but real blood squirting out into the audience on your adoring fans is a nice touch once in a great while.

Be prepared to be slandered by the pretty ones in the drag community. They will use and abuse your name to everyone, and honestly there is no such thing as bad PR, so let them talk shit. Eventually people will wonder why you are so tragic. Your friends will salvage your reputation, defending your unique and cleverness.

The last little note I will leave you with until the next issue, is the source of your inspiration.

The power you wield is great and should be treated with respect. If you let ego and pride cloud your projection, you will soon find how lonely it feels in the land of misfit toys. Try to be an innovator, a creative creator, and a damsel in distress, but don't play into the hands of the lion's den. The bitches with tiaras and beaded gowns will only book you in their shows for a few side laughs among themselves, a costume change, and most of all, they will not pay you well.

Try to make nice and hang with other Dumpster Divas to become part of the growing sensation as an original. Never settle for needing anything but your own talent. It is, and always will be, your only friend in the end. Who wants to play with someone who is looking for pity parties to drink empty teacups of pretend tea with teddy bears dressed in pretty dresses, when you can come out dressed like "Godzilla" and stomp out all of the tourists?

The audience will in turn, throw their hard earned money to you as gluttons for punishment to continuously watch you perform. Well, until I type again, try to stay sane, but look incredibly insane, and become "she who is the drag queen inside of you," unleash her!

TTFN. (Ta Ta for now).

Lady Jasmine, Scott Stebane, and Neely O'Hara
Miss North America International 2012 Pageant
Kenosha, Wisconsin
Photo Credit: Amanda Lay

Anastasia Fallon and Jay Santana

Official Drag Handbook

Photo By:
Vincent J. Wiercinski

Send "one single"
picture to
DRAG411.com

Note your name,
location, and the
person taking the photo.

DRAG411's DRAG Memorial page on DRAG411.com

Mis Sadistic
The thing that excited me the most about wearing girls' clothing was how glamorous it made me look and feel. I was blessed with a talent to make myself transform into stars like Cher and many others.

Lady Tajma Hall
I have always been my mother's child, and wearing women's clothing made me feel closer to my mother. I would always look in the mirror and think that I looked just like my mother. My mother was a natural woman, and only wore lip gloss and mascara....I tried that but realized I wanted to wear a little more!

Jocelyn Summers
Nothing, it is tight, binding, and uncomfortable, especially the shoes.

Jade Shanell
Being in drag is just fun. You get to bring a character to life and get to get people around you to have fun too. But, I do admit, I am a shoe whore, higher the better. If they make it, I can walk in it. (wink)

Kori Stevens
There isn't anything exciting about wearing women's clothing. The exciting thing is being able to entertain audiences. It is uncomfortable.

Horchata
Corsets and wigs. The girl just need to come out and it makes you feel feminine. Let's not forget the heels.

Michael Wilson
It wasn't the clothes and never is, that is a huge misconception about showgirls. It is all about the applause.

Naomi Wynters
I wasn't exactly excited to try on girl's clothing, but being the size that I am I didn't have a choice. The only thing that excites me about being in girl's clothing is the audience reaction, the illusion that is being passed forth from the clothing, makeup, wigs. Other than that, it's a hassle, but the fit is usually amazing :)

Deva DaVyne
Cocktail Dresses, Skirts, and heels! I'm obsessed with my legs, so anything that I could wear to show off my long legs always excited me, and still does.

Stephen Brooks
Excited???? Nothing...I got great legs, and can create some good looking cleavage, but it's just for the show...

Felina Cashmere
As a drag queen, nothing excites me in the sexual context, but as far as creating the look of a woman, being able to wear it better than an actual woman is my vanity. Plus, I have hot legs. :)

Maxine Padlock
As a big guy I got some nasty glares sometimes, but as a woman I got all the attention and compliments. I love making my own stuff now too. This way I can push the limits and really have them.

Sybil Storm
I love attention.

Mike Asterman
It was more for the entertaining of the people than it was the girls clothes.

Amanda Bone
Wigs and heels were what excited me. I was soooo excited to wear wigs.

Selina Kyle
The creativity, and just the feeling of this new person that I was able to unleash upon the world, without holding back.

Misty Eyes
I love the LONG HAIR... I used to be jealous of girls on swingsets. When they went up their hair would touch the ground... or when they were jogging in gym and their pony tails would sway.... but I also LOVE LONG FLOWY Skirts / dresses etc... that is what got me addicted...

Diamond Dunhill
Shoes, heels were not an instant hit with me. It wasn't even the bra, or Nerf Balls cut in half for tits. It would have to be lining my lips with liner, lipstick and gloss Accentuating my trademark "Smile." AND subsequently "The Diamond Dunhill Open Mouth"! :D

Miss Gigi
I just think it was the attention, and the fun I have and had with it, because it is something you don't see every day. It causes looks and questions....and people want to come talk to you...and I love talking

to people and just being around them. Plus, with doing it I could do HUGE hair...and wear eight inch platform shoes most women are scared to wear...but I love it...

Makanoe
I just loved the variety and colors and all the fucking shoes these bitches had to choose from. We, as men, had suits, and ties, and flats...It's exciting to dress in a ball gown just because.

Diedra Windsor Walker
Oh I loved furs and I loved the jewels and I loved being glamorous. I wanted and still love the 1940's and 1950's style. It's so glamorous and just fabulous. I love the hairstyles...the Victory Buns.

Melissa Morgan
It was fun. It was a chance to step out of my world into Melissa's World but even know they are the same world in a little way, although they are worlds apart.

Kiki LaFlare Santangilo
The glamor was what pulled me into the world of Female Impersonation. I also loved the heels, the walk, the wig, and the fact that I felt beautiful. Being an overweight guy can be tough, but when I put on that tight dress and 5 inch heels everyone seemed to notice me. I had a figure and I actually started getting compliments. I felt gorgeous.

Adrian Leigh
A way to "cover" my identity (and youth) to get into the bars at age 16. At the time, Drags are usually not carded.

Anastasia Fallon
I always had a flare for the stage, but never found much connection with the roles I played in my early years. Finding myself in these female roles was just more exciting, and for me, more relative to the life I was living. Something about portraying a character within a character is so much more intriguing to me.

Champagne T. Bordeaux
After 20 years, I'm more excited getting out of them. I'm a jeans and sweats chick, so really a nice hoodie gets me excited, flip flops, sports bra etc. All the other outfits come with stress, will they like it, will it all stay on, can I do a high kick in this outfit??? Stress, stress, stress, short on excitement.

Ororo
I just like to confuse people.

Brianna Lee
Back in the day, It was all about the attention.

Vivika D'Angelo
Confusing people, but even when i am not dressed, people mistake me for a girl, even with a 5 o'clock shadow, go figure.

Kier
Cher.

Toni DaVyne
I grew up listening to a lot of Barbara Streisand, and watching her movies. So, when i started dressing as a girl i was excited to be as pretty as she was!

Jessica Jade
I loved the hair!

Amy DeMilo
I'm not even sure, but my goodness, my parents had a hard time with me wanting to be in my sister's clothes.

Michelle Tatum
The fact that I could transform, and look totally different.

Pandora DeStrange
I always preferred girl's clothes over boy's clothes when I was little...much to my parents dismay!

Shealita BaBay
BIG DICKS

Wendy G Kennedy
The attention I get, the compliments, although I love costumes, so think of me as Bugs Bunny.

Beverly LaSalle
The thing that excited me the most about dressing up was the fact that first, I was able to wear all these amazing clothes, and second, that I was able to be what I felt was ME!

Jade Jolie
Women have much more options and a wider variety of fashion choices. It's exciting to experiment with a different array of styles.

Jami Micheals
I never really enjoyed wearing women's clothes as much as I loved the stage, the spotlight, and all the attention I got.

LeAnna Love
The thrill of the performance. The idea that I was gonna be someone else for a couple of hours.

Dmentia Divinyl
The shock value to others. I always felt beautiful on the inside and out, and to me it was just another way of natural expression.

Geraldine Queencabaret
The feeling of happiness while doing it is what exited me.

Alisa Summers
I really enjoy the shopping aspect of it. I am definitely addicted to spending money. Then, taking the things you bought, and piecing them together to create a final look is the best.

Demonica da Bomb
The prospect of performing. Always been a performer!

Juwana Jackson
I don't think it was the wearing women's clothing, it was the fact that I was creating a whole new identity, and in this identity I could be the person I always wanted to be. Popular, a celebrity, a very
open, fun, wild animal person, which is completely opposite from my male side.

Crystal Belle
It excited me that I felt like a new person when I put on women's clothing. I felt like I was someone else, someone beautiful and confident. I knew then, that I love feeling confident and sexy because it feels like I can do anything! When I am Crystal, I can do anything, say anything, be anything that I want to be.

Esme Russell
I wouldn't say I was excited. I am transgender, it was what needed to be done. I was not happy living as a boy.

PurrZsa Kyttyn
I always picked out my sister's clothes for Christmas based on what I wanted to wear, and I always liked the feel of panty hose

Lacey Lynn Taylors
Nothing sexual about drag. There is absolutely no pleasure to be found in duct tape, hip pads and corseting. It was merely the thought that I made both a pretty boy and a pretty girl.

Eunyce Raye
I got to express a part of my personality that usually I did not get to do.

Joey Brooks
Attention that I didn't get dressed as a boy.

Kenneth Blake
Money!

Glitz Glam
I've always admired HIGH HEELS and CORSETS.

Angela Dodd
Women's clothes are simply more fun. They have so many more options, and trends are easier to stay up on. I love seeing a well-dressed woman walking down the street or shopping or something. That said, I am honest when I tell you that wearing store bought, off-the-rack, 'real' women's clothing is not something that I generally get excited about. I love being in front of an audience- I get extremely excited about performing and wearing the costumes that I've made for stage and the character I play.

Teri Courtney (RIP)
The excitement has always been in the glamor for me.

Nairobi V. D'Viante
How I looked when I danced in them. I wasn't performing on the stage, but I would dance all night long full speed ahead so I had to have some cute threads.

Lady Liemont
Women have always had more options when it comes to clothing. I enjoy the transformation, and the ability to wear almost anything.

Patrice Knight
I was more excited about the looks I received while dressed as a girl, more so than the actual wearing of the clothes. Patrice was able to do and say things that Michael never would.

Raven Manniac
Not a DAMN thing about wearing it... it was the chance to be someone else. Not the clothes, but the persona...

Twat Sisters
All the dates it got us!!

Pussy Lahoot
I was a plain, shy boy...being a pretty girl, I felt the rush of being able to do anything. I was always attracted to boys, but since I didn't know what gay was, much less know any other gays in Flagstaff, Arizona at that time, it was my way of getting good attention from boys.

Jade Daniels
I just love fashion, and I think men's clothes are boring. How many different ways can you wear a t-shirt, polo, or button down shirt? But with girl's clothes, your options are LIMITLESS!

Rickie Lee
Actually,nothing. What excited me was the performing, the applause, the recognition, the stature, and the ability to pull it off for intrigue.

Raquel Payne
It was always all about the shows, and female impersonation that made me excited to wear girl's clothing.

Vegas Platinum
It was more of the art of female impersonation than that of putting on a dress that inspired me to do what I do.

Monique Michaels
I like the attention of entertaining. For me, it's not so much about the clothes, male or female, but about entertaining. Being on stage, having all eyes on you, and the energy of the crowd.

Jaeda Fuentes
It wasn't necessarily the fact that I was wearing girl's clothing. It's more of the entertainment factor that I love about drag.

BukkakeBlaque London St James
The Heels and the Heels.

Dee Gregory
As a young boy I was always fascinated with disguises and costumes. Two movies redirected my choice of costumes; William Castle's "HOMICIDAL" and "FREEBIE AND THE BEAN" I saw the seamless illusions and thought, "WOW, the ultimate disguise, being the other sex." (gender wasn't yet in my vocabulary).

TotiYanah Diamond
I think it was the way they felt. Girl clothes seem to be more delicate then guys. I think I loved that factor a lot. And, the way they are made to fit a body type. The sex appeal it gives off was also a good factor for me.

Conundrum
I have always loved the designs, colors , and bold looks that are incorporated into Women's clothing. I have always thought that Men's clothes are kind of dull and boring, although that has changed a lot with time. I still think that Women's clothing is much more eccentric!

Lisa Carr
I don't know about everyone else, but as a professional entertainer, there's no sexual excitement in wearing women's clothes. In fact, it's a lot of work and the shoes and corsets can actually be painful. My wardrobe isn't "women's' clothes" they are professional costumes that do not resemble anything a typical woman would wear. Most of us create an over-the-top illusion.

Barbra Herr
It was just natural for me.

Katrina Starr
Nothing, it hurts!!!! Well the shoes hurt, and the bra feels weird

Leilani Masters
The transformation into my character. The acknowledgement from audiences or your fans, and strangers that you have somehow convinced with your over all look and the personality that goes with it and they are intrigued and want to know or see more.

**This is only a copy of the actual Magazine created in 2012.
Except for DRAG411.com, all email addresses and links
are no longer active or available.**

Jenna Telia
I thought that maybe I would get a straight guy to have an interest in me. So far, I have had their hands up and down me and they hardly can see the guy side of me, I guess I was blessed with the proper assets, my tits look real with the cleavage i got, and my ass looks like you could eat your way to China. I guess straight guys only like those things, so I am barking up the right tree. Keep fondling me whenever you see me in public .As long as your hot, I don't mind!

Aime Jean
I feel like I'm another person, another personality, like a super hero, I leave my life behind every time I transform into AIME.

Nostalgia Notanotherrerun Ronin
Accessorizing and creating the illusion enough to be not recognizable. I work close to where I perform, so if I let down for a minute, it could affect my career.

Dr. J.
I have always felt more comfortable in "boys wear," and performing as Dr. J gives me the opportunity to just relax and let that part of me out to play.

Stefon Royce Iman
I feel excited to wear boy clothes because I felt comfortable. I felt like a tomboy. When I wore them I got comments on wow he is cute. They had no idea I was a female, so that was a great feeling.

Butt Wiser
They were comfortable and roomie. I looked stylish.

Pimp Daddy (also performs as Lady Chabli)
I love wearing zoot suits and as Sassy Chablis, I love wearing gowns.

Papi Chulo
It excites Papi Chulo to dress up and go out because it feels RIGHT for that moment. I feel very masculine inside and that is what makes my Papi Chulo Image pop out, CONFIDENCE and STRUT.

Daisha Monet'
What excited me on dressing up in drag was the fact that it allows you to be someone else and feel good about it. I grew up in a very small county town that is still today stuck on race and homosexual issues. I always dreamt of being a famous red carpet superstar. As you can see, I'm not

there yet. So, until then, when I'm in drag and on stage, I consider that to be my personal red carpet moment.

Insure your comments are in the next issue:
At Drag411.com
Deadline for the Summer Issue is June 12, 2102
Or just click the colored link.

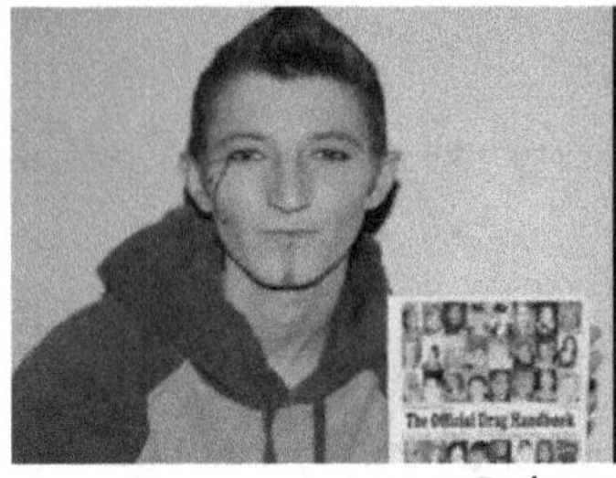

Logan Dale and Britney Houston-Boheme
Official Drag Handbook

The first rule to writing is to write about what you know. My column is called "Keeping It Old School" and I know a lot about that!

The best place to start is the beginning. I have been a drag performer for thirty-one years. I have called Ohio my home for most of that time. I did spend two years in Nashville Tennessee and six years in

Orlando, Florida. I got my start in a small club in Warren, Ohio called the Office; it's no longer in business.

I was a bartender at the office. Occasionally the bar would book drag entertainers, mostly local performers, but every so often, we booked a big name act. I remember the first "big name" entertainer we booked was Odessa Brown. He was billed as the "World's Largest Female Impersonator," and at 700 lbs., and he was. I was star struck the first time I watched Odessa perform! Odessa sang live!

It was something I never seen a drag performer before her. I knew right then I wanted to perform, and wanted to do it live. Over the next three decades, I had the honor of performing all over this great nation as a live act.

I have always had great inspiration throughout my career and one of my biggest influences was a performer named Mag Reiley. I met Mag in the early 80's at a club called "The Troubadour Lounge" in Youngstown Ohio. Miss Reiley hosted a talent night. I decided to enter it, and it became the night of the birth of Denise Russell!

My life changed after winning the talent show, I had the drag bug. Over the next few months, I began to know Mag on a personal level. The gay community called Mag, "The Mother of Youngstown," and she was. I learned so much from Mag over the time I knew her. She had been a drag performer in New York City in the late forty's. I was so intrigued by her stories of the old days. Back then, all drag performers sang live.

There were no sound systems in the nightclubs, only a combo band, so all the queens sang. It was not until the mid-fifties that lip sync came into the picture. Mag always told me I was a throwback to the old days, and I should keep performing live. She told me that my voice was my ticket to great things.

As I traveled from city to city, I had the great fortune to meet some wonderful old school performers, people like Billie Boots, Miss P, Chris Cross, Charlie Brown and Tula. I know the younger generations will not know some of these names, but these are the performers that paved the way for all of us. I think it is important to know our Gay history, and to pass it along to the younger performers. Over the coming issues of SPOTLIGHT TODAY Magazine I am going to profile some of the old school performers and share their stories with you.

In my next column, I am going to do an in depth interview with "Tula" the Empress of Ft. Wayne. Tula is now in her seventies and still performing.

Until next time, remember to keep our history alive, it is important to know where we came from to understand where we are going.

Thirtieth Anniversary Celebration of
After Dark Night Club in Ft. Wayne, Indiana
Front Row: Denise Russell, Tula, Chelsea Pearl.
Back Row: Twila Star and Darcel Stevens
Photo Credit: Jay McLane

The Rock
Phoenix, AZ

Sherry Vine, Joey Arias,
And Olivia Gardens
Photo By: Vincent J. Wiercinski

Another
Moment with
Maggie
Magenta Alexandria Dupree
@SpotlightTodayMagazine.com

o   Perseverance is defined as commitment, hard work, patience, endurance.
o   Perseverance is being able to bear difficulties calmly and without complaint.
o   Perseverance is trying again and again.
o   Perseverance is one of the three P's that make up a drag persona.

To persevere means never give up, and try your best to succeed. Every time you save money, to sacrifice to buy something, or when you spend hours practicing your music, you are showing perseverance. Perseverance in drag means to work hard at being the best at your craft, to try over and over until that craft is perfected.

Each time you rehearse your lip-syncing techniques, or your sexy runway walk, you are persevering in drag. Each hour you spend stoning that next pageant gown, you are persevering drag. When it comes to patience, it is definitely a virtue; drag is not any easy craft to persevere.

Commitment is necessary in order to succeed. Without commitment you simply waste your time. Hard work with commitment definitely pays off with success. Endurance is being able to handle whatever comes your way. Most people define drag as a drama-filled environment. Being able to endure that drama, and get past it, is perseverance in drag. In drag, perseverance means not complaining.

Beauty is pain. Complaining about pain will get you "read" by a fellow queen, and it is not going to help you persevere and perfect your craft. I have been in the business for a decade and experienced the best and the worst of drag. I know perseverance and way to achieve it.

Professionalism and Performance are the other two P's of drag, but I will discuss those in future issues of SPOTLIGHT TODAY Magazine. Being professional on stage and in the dressing room is a very important part of persevering. Showing hard work pays off in a performance is persevering as well.

Overall, perseverance encompasses every aspect of a drag persona. It spectrum includes transformation, designing, rehearsing, interacting with guests, and performing. Perseverance in drag is the first, and most important, part of the perfection of your craft: the art of drag.

Perseverance determines the other two P's of the drag persona.

This has been a Moment with Maggie.

Tim Ferguson and Bob Taylor
Official Drag Handbook

The Stud
San Francisco, CA
All About Evil Pre-Show

Peaches Christ, Jenna Telia,
and Pandora DeStrange

Photo By: Glenn Storm

**Horchetta and The Twat Sisters
Official Drag Handbook**

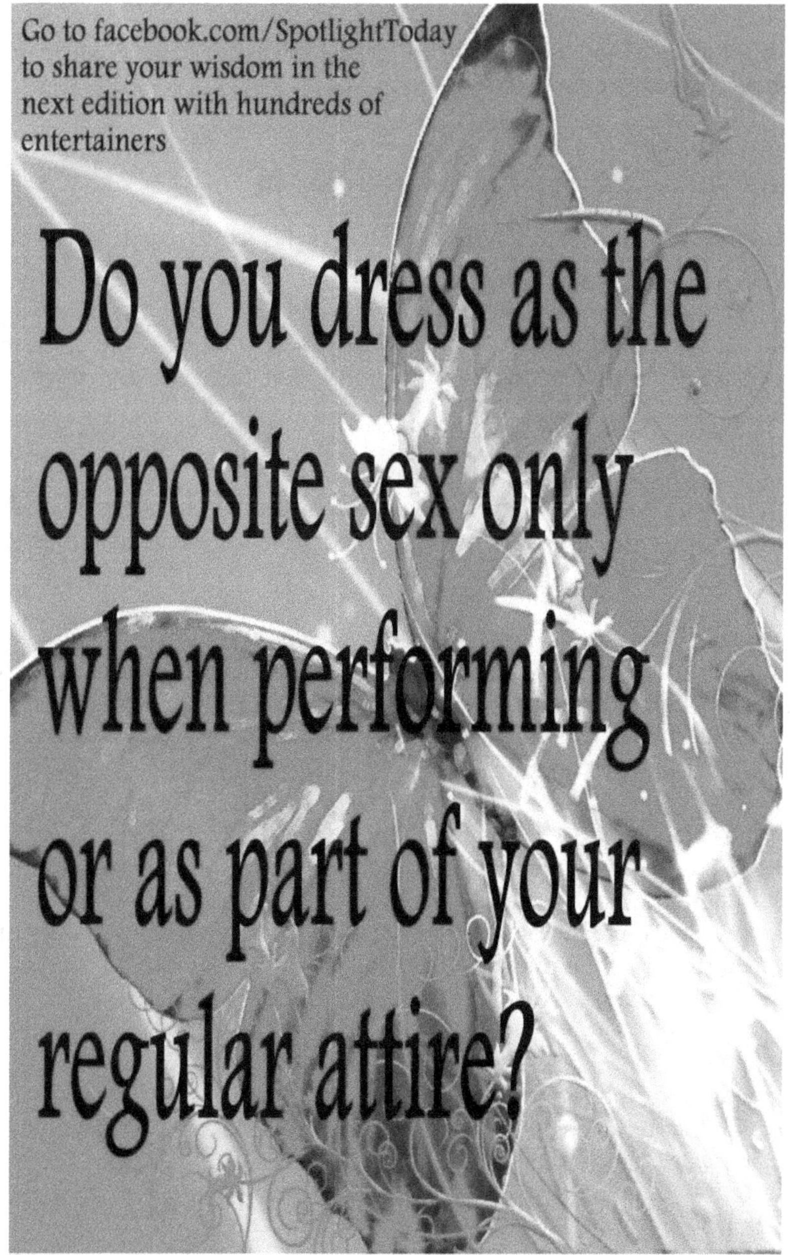

Kenneth Blake
Only when on stage, or promoting an event.

Barbra Seville
Only for a show. And usually only on stage. I will hang out for a while after a show, but never before. It's not my thing.

Vinnie Marconi
Beard is for performing, my attire stays the same!!

Jayson Rave
I dress in male attire both on and off stage. My name is the same both on and off stage. The only thing that changes is my last name. The only time I wear any kind of makeup is when I am performing, I poked myself in the eyeball with mascara last night!! And, I only have facial hair when I glue it on.

Felina Cashmere:
Only during shows and events. I live a life as a guy, I have to, and I like drawing the line between the two personas, its more intriguing during the unveiling.

Alexis De La Mer:
I ONLY dress up for Performances and FABULOUS nights out. Once I saw my friends in NYC dressing up in Drag, it was SOMETHING i had to do, i was a Former Model, Comedian, and LOVE Makeup and costume design, SOOOOO it was ONLY natural I roll.

Maxine Padlock:
I like to dress fishy or like an all gurls slumber party when I am going to the bar to perform. Then I prepare for my numbers backstage and give it to them when I step out. Sometimes I like to go to drag functions dressed up very pretty on a little drag side. Depending on the occasion I can tone it down or tune it up!

Daphne Ferraro
I only dress for performance purposes. In the past, I may have stayed in drag for a little bit longer if a cute guy was into "Daphne". Tranny Chasers are always so damn hot.

Horchata
Performances and also when I feel like it, meaning when I wanna have fun like clubbing or to the bar. Sometimes I might wanna be a girl for the nite and just do something different.

Michael Wilson
Okay - performances. You have several degrees. Cross dressers, the ones who get turned on my wearing women's clothes; Bar queens, they run around the bar usually talking trash thinking they are fabulous; and showgirls, self-explanatory

Trixie Scott
Only performances. I love who I am, and I'm never going to change it. Being a Drag Queen is theatre to me. It's portraying the idea of someone you are not. I will never dress in drag outside of a performance setting.

Naomi Wynters
I dress only as/during a performance. When I plan on performing, that time I have set aside to be at the bar/club to socialize, take pictures perform whatever is set for the bar. I generally change when i get home. I am a man, I love my life.

Deva DaVyne
Performances/special events and for nights out with friends. I live my life as a guy, but I do dress up and get paint a face on from time to time, just to have fun with friends and meet people. For me, when people meet you off the stage, and you actually talk to people and get to know them, they respect you more as a performer/person.

Stephen Brooks
My female character, "BJ Stephens" is just that...a character. If I need to be "in character" for something, then I will put on my costume, otherwise, I socialize, and live as a man.

Mike Asterman
for a while i was 24-7, that was for about 10years.

Amanda Bone
I live my life as a man. I only dress up for shows

Jenna Telia
I only dress up as "Jenna Telia" for promotion, and for shock value. I have no reason to be a girl, as I am handsome as a boy. Drag gives me a chance to transform and be someone else. To be bitchy and rude whenever i feel like it and i never have to apologize, but it is all in good fun, and I really never disappoint people. I always take their picture, make funny faces, and get people involved that are shy. I think it also helps me with the fact that I don't drink alcohol. Being a drag queen opens the door to my inhibitions and lets me be a freak, I don't need any substance to lubricate me while in

drag as I am full of myself and feeling up the boys. It's fun, and I am not ashamed of any part of it. TRY IT, it has helped me be myself in more ways than one.

Aime Jean
I dress up as AIME as I need, sometimes just for show. This past year I started to attend events, and people take a lot of pictures of me, so i like that. I'm starting to dress up for as many events as I can.

Selina Kyle
To me, the art of DRAG is like Theater. I go to the bar or club as a guy, I get into character, and then when I'm done with the show, or the night, the makeup and character are put away until next time.

Misty Eyes
I live my life as a man... and I do Drag for work... but once in drag (like tonight I'm doing a gig in Miami from 7-11), I'll stay dressed up and spend the rest of my evening as Misty and go out somewhere after, etc....

Diamond Dunhill
I'm a boy in the day, gurl at night. No additions, no subtractions. I have stood by that since day one Of Diamond Dunhill, September 19, 1999.

Daisha Monet'
I have no feelings or desire to become a woman, or have any work done. I'm perfectly fine with creating my alter ego from my cosmetic bag. I'm a drag queen, not a tranny. I live my life daily as a male. I only don my drag gear when needed for bookings and what-not. To me, a drag queen is someone that is overly creative, and needs an outlet to vent their talent. A tranny is someone who mentally thinks that they were born in the wrong body, and in my case, that's not the case.

Amanda Love
No longer performing at the moment, but when I was, you only saw Amanda when she was at the club, not out and about, in town.

Miss Gigi
I do it when I have shows, and when I have to do something and want to support another drag queen. I will dress up for them as well for a benefit show, or just to be supportive.

Diedra Windsor Walker
Only as a performer. I consider myself a female impersonator/entertainer, and this is an art-form.

Makanoe
I am a man. I dress as a man with the occasional adornment of women's jeans, because I love the cut and the way it makes my real ass look. I only dress in full face for the stage, or doing stand-up. Performing. Period.

Melissa Morgan
Most of the time it is when I perform! I do get dressed up to go out and hang out with friends and such.

Nostalgia Notanotherrerun Ronin
I enjoy drag as a performance outlet for my creativity. Ninety percent of my time in drag is in front of the mirror at home, perfecting my craft. There is a misconception that people only dress in drag because of a desire to become the opposite gender. I'm fortunate enough to have recently found an entire group that feels as adverse to this as I do.

Joshua Myers
I dress in women's clothing or my drag costumes (because let's face it - women don't, and wouldn't, wear what I wear on stage). But, do not be deceived. When I am off stage, I'm all sorts of MAN. I perform for entertainment and money. I will occasionally do it for charity, or for a benefit, but drag is a business

Pimp Daddy (also performs as Lady Chabli)
I dress in men's attire both on and off stage. My name only changes on stage to Pimp Daddy

Kiki LaFlare Santangilo
I dress in Drag ONLY when I'm performing. When my song is over, I'm back stage taking off the makeup and my outfit. I walk in the club as a man, I get ready back stage, and I leave the club as a man. Drag is for entertainment purposes only for me. I've had several men ask if I would dress as a woman all the time so we could date, but I turned them down. I'm not into that. Drag is not a sexual thing for me.

Adrian Leigh
Only for performances

Dr. J.
My every day dress is kind of unisex and comfortable, not too girlie and not too masculine and my demeanor is the same. Performance is when I bind the chest, pack my undies, wear facial hair and my demeanor/attitude changes too~

Anastasia Fallon
I like to blur some gender lines and go with a little bit of an androgynous flare from time to time, but these days, Anastasia is limited to performances & photo shoots.

Champagne T. Bordeaux
Simply put I live female, I dress for work. The difference is going to the grocery takes about a good 10 minutes from bathroom to car, going to a gig bumps that time from 10 minutes to 45. I wouldn't get that question in my regular daily life, only in the community which sees me primarily as a female impersonator. I am an illusionist, an impersonator is being someone you're not. I'm me at the market, and I'm me on stage. It's the illusion that changes, not the person.

Mis Sadistic
I only dress as a female when I am performing. It is a lot of work, and takes me about an hour and a half to put myself together. The majority of the time is spent on my makeup. I take great pains in making myself look real, especially if I am impersonating a celebrity, like Cher or Amy Winehouse. When I am done with the show, I can't wait to get it all off. I feel like a Claymation doll. I do female impersonation, I do not want to be a woman, there is a very big difference. Keep in mind there are so many degrees of people who dress. None are more or less important than the others when it comes to individual feelings. Please remember everyone should be respected, no matter what category they fall under. Drag, Trans, Cross dresser etc.....

Patricia Mason
I have absolutely no desire to be a woman. I enjoy being masculine and being a man. I do enjoy putting on a show, creating a character, and bringing that person to life. Being a female illusionist takes me from one extreme to the other.

Lady Tajma Hall
I am a female, and dress as a female every day! I look at society through a female's eyes, and cope the same way! I become a female impersonator when it is time for me to do a show or pageant. Some people think it is easier for me because I live as a female. I wish someone would tell my body that!

Jocelyn Summers
I am a boy in the day. At one time i had considered becoming a transsexual, but I think I was more in it for the attention that Jocelyn got. I learned quickly that is not the right reason to transition. A true Transsexual

has a desire, and need, from an early age to be the opposite sex. I did not, I was so in need of positive attention that I thought that would be an easy way for me to get it on a regular basis.. It's not, it's a hard road to take. I don't envy a lot of girls out there, their road is not an easy one.

Jade Shanell
I only dress as Lady during performances, pageants, or going out to watch drag shows. All other days I'm just a regular guy working during the day, trying to enjoy life with loved ones.

Brianna Lee
I only dress to perform, or to go "hang out with the girls". I dress 100% as a man all other times. Time and cost is everything.

Kori Stevens
I live my life as a man. I only dress as a woman when I am performing or competing. I have no desire to be a woman, or anything else other than myself. My stage persona is just that.

Ororo
It all depends. At first, I only dressed up for shows, but I've always felt more comfortable as a woman, so i found a medium. Drag is drag, use more makeup, more hair, more everything. Why not do it big? Every day living, I'm just me. Most of the time people think I'm a "dyke" , not to offend anyone.

Vivika D'Angelo
I dress as a female when I am either performing or of course competing or when I go out to a club once in a while.

Kier
It depends on my mood. I don't go out to the mall in drag though.=

Toni DaVyne
I go out a lot in drag to promote myself and network and bring in new people to the clubs. I only shop for drag IN drag, because I feel like that is the only way you'll know for sure if it'll fit right and look good with the look you're going for.

Jessica Jade
I don't do it as part of regular attire, so for me it's only for performance or special events, usually. However, from time to time I do go out just to be out in face.

Amy DeMilo
I do not always wear makeup, but always dress as a woman!

Michelle Tatum
I only dress up for "SHOWS/Performances" ....I have found that I have more respect for actual women or people that are transgendered if I only keep my dressing up to "WORK related things"...Remember, it's called SHOW BUSINESS for a reason.

Pandora DeStrange
I throw on some drag whenever the mood strikes me! It puts a little pep in my step and some glide in my stride!

Shealita BaBay
I am a PROUD REPUBLICAN CHRISTIAN WOMAN!

Conundrum
I live as a Male. Drag is my Job, so the only time I dress as a female is during performances, or outings to the nightclubs, I feel that you can promote yourself more dressed as your drag persona when going out to clubs.

Lisa Carr
The only time I dress as a "female" is to perform in my female persona. I'm very much a guy, but a theatrical guy. Drag is a means to an end. There is a huge difference between cross dressers and drag queens. Cross dressers enjoy dressing in women's' clothing to feel feminine, and sometimes gain a sexual excitement from the experience. Drag Queens dress in "female" attire to put on a show, create a character illusion, and entertain an audience. Most times a cross dresser's audience is simply a mirror at home and it's a more personal thing. Drag Queens are out to show who they can become, not necessarily who they really are.

Lady Clover Honey
I dress and express myself as a female in all kinds of occasions, especially parties and social gatherings, not just performance.

Makayla Rose Devine
Only as a performer.

Barbra Herr
I am, and have been trans for the majority of my adult life.

Katrina Starr
Mostly performances. I want to start going to bars in drag, to promote myself as a queen, to get my name out there.

Wendy G Kennedy
I`m a Drag Queen, I only dress in women's garments for shows, although I`ve been pulled over by Cops on four different times while in drag, and they treated me so nice. Best of all, I didn`t get a ticket. I told my wife I`m considering the option of dressing like that 24/7. That will make me a Transvestite... Right?

Beverly LaSalle
The only time I dress like a woman is when I am on stage. It takes at least an hour to put myself together, and I couldn't see myself doing it on a daily basis. There are so many different labels for men that wear woman's clothing, be it cross dresser, transvestite, etc. However, (and no disrespect is meant by this) but someone that lives their life as a woman is on a different level than a female impersonator. They live that life 24/7 as opposed to someone such as me, that does it for entertainment.

Tabatha Lovall
I only dress up when I'm going to perform. Once in a while, I'll put a frock on for a party or social gathering.

Jami Micheals
Only in performances. I'm very comfortable being a man who entertains as a female, but I always am supportive of whatever decisions my sisters decide to make for their own lives

LeAnna Love
Only during performance.

Cartier Paris
Only during performances. I like to have down time.

Dmentia Divinyl
I perform live in shows and on film, in movies made by my company. I believe that in order to get in touch with who you are as a performer or impersonator, you must walk a mile in the shoes. I do wear clothing sometimes that makes me feel more like my character, even out of drag, but I am not a transvestite. I am totally turned off by being hit on dressed up like a female, although I have been turned on by seeing guys who look like a woman, but no boner, just think they are sexy.

Geraldine Queencabaret
I do it when I work. I also do it for fun when I am off and feel like it. On top of that, I promote myself and socialize from my fraud queen persona..

Brandon M. Caten
I only dress as a female when it is time to go on stage! All other times, I have found it easier to just be me!

Alisa Summers
I live as a man during the day, and perform in drag at night for work. On a regular daily basis, I have a job and dress in my regular male attire.

Demonica da Bomb
Just for a performance. In drag in the club, period.

Juwana Jackson
When I first started, I dressed as a woman to go out, to perform, to go to gay bars and straight bars. I thought it was FUN to go to ladies night at a straight bar and have guys hitting on me. Of course, I was naive and thank God I wasn't hurt. Now I only dress up to perform, or when there is a special event like a pageant, and I want to be seen.

Esme Russell
I have lived as a female since I was 15. When I get in high drag to perform, I add more makeup and hair and amplify my female persona to an extreme level, so that I appear more like a drag queen .

Crystal Belle
I wear it when I need to. That being said, I am a female impersonator, so I wear it when I am impersonating; for a performance, a photo shoot, a special event. I love the thrill of getting dressed up and becoming someone else, so that happens pretty frequently. During the day, however, I have a professional career, so I can't always dress like a woman during those times. I have to maintain a level of masculine professionalism during the day.

PurrZsa Kyttyn
I'm a performance only girl, although I will wander out in face to a bar to mingle, or to do photos. I do not live as a woman. I am not a TS.

Lacey Lynn Taylors
Lacey Lynn Taylors lives in my closet for the most part. Drag is really a very small part of my life. I enjoy being a man, but drag gives me an escape from my everyday life. It is kind of therapeutic in the means that I can be

someone else and act in ways I never would as Eric. As far as changing my demeanor, I change very little. The use of foam pads and breast forms give the hourglass figure, but my voice does not change, nor does my personality. I just tend to be slightly more outgoing as Lacey.

Eunyce Raye
Only for performances. I enjoy being regular me when out of drag.

Joey Brooks
Only during performances or when I go the bar to market myself.

Glitz Glam
I'm a Drag Queen, I do not impersonate other females. I wear elaborate costumes with feminine accessories & I do it to entertain people.

Shawn Kelly
Only for performances. I live my life as a man-thing.

Jade Daniels
I only dress up in drag for performances, charity events, or big promotional events. Drag/Female Impersonating is a business for me. It's like putting on a uniform for work. So, if there is no booking fee involved, raising money for a good cause, or networking to gain future opportunities...then there is no "Jade Daniels".

Barbra Seville
Only for a show, and usually only on stage. I will hang out for a while after a show, but never before. It's not my thing.

Ashleigh Cooley
I actually am a pre-op transsexual as well as performing drag. I've been on hormones for 4+ years now, and am looking forward to having GRS in the near future. I have been a full time girl for 5 months now.
*This reply was in the start of 2011.

Rickie Lee
Only for performing, unless otherwise required. I've been in weddings which required I be in drag, Pride Events which were not only performing but being in drag. But, mostly just for performing. That keeps it special for me. I have no desire to be a woman totally.

Raquel Payne
I only dress as a female for shows.

Vegas Platinum
Only for stage and going out to clubs. I couldn't imagine getting ready every morning. DRAG IS PLAIN AND SIMPLY UNCOMFORTABLE!

Monique Michaels
I only dress as a woman when I am performing, or doing certain social functions. My daily life is male. I feel, for me personally, that the illusion and persona are all for stage.

Jaeda Fuentes
I only dress as a female when I am doing shows or out promoting myself.

BukkakeBlaque London St James
Only for the stage!

Dee Gregory
As my regular attire, no. But beyond the stage, yes. See 'Dee' is a character I enjoy creating and bringing to life, and she has become more and more visible in regular public venues over time. I do try to dress appropriately for the situation, of course.

TotiYanah Diamond
I love to dress up when I feel like it, even if it's just to take pictures at home. I love the whole process of getting ready. I like to go out in drag at times just with the girls. I have so much fun doing it. It's a way I can express myself.

Angela Dodd
Dude looks like a lady... only to perform and such. I'm a gay man who enjoys men who are into men. Angela Dodd is a character that I play. She is not a real person. If not entertaining, I'm Jim all the way.

Afeelya Bunz
I have been performing for 8 years, and this is the only time I dress up

Teri Courtney (RIP)
I am a full time woman, have been since I was 14. I just wear a lot less makeup to Walmart!
Nairobi V. D'Viante
Only as a performer. I live the life of a common man. I work a day job, have a nephew, and am the oldest son. Drag to me is my craft, something I take a great deal of pride in and approach with the utmost respect.

Lady Liemont
I only dress when I perform, or on special events at the bar. I enjoy being a boy.

Patrice Knight
I only dressed as a female when I was performing or trying to get work. I would go out and let bar owners see what I looked like. DRAG has always been about Entertaining for me. I am not sexually aroused by being in DRAG.

Babette Schwartz
I put on a dress when I am being paid! Drag is about performing for me.

Raven Manniac
DRAG is performance. I am a Man. I live as a man, and the woman is a character I become for a short time - now, once in a very rare while.

Twat Sisters
Only to perform and club hop! We enjoy doing it to see the look and smiles that it creates.

Pussy Lahoot
At age fifty I'm still sometimes called ma'am, even when I'm doing the boy thing. I do still love to go out and party in full tilt boogie drag; otherwise... I'm just Kevin.

Stefon Royce Iman
I dress like a man for performance because of the hair on my face. I still have my tomboy style, and dress like a boy from time to time. I also like to stay in tune with my feminine side. My dress attire as a tomboy is totally different from me dressing as a male impersonator. I can say both attires are similar, but are different. I don't walk around with hair on my face, or a bulge in my pants, so that is the difference.

Trixie LaRue
Like I said, I'm a boy that is a boy who does female impersonation as an art. I like to go to the show as a boy, and almost always leave as a boy. I have a theater undergraduate degree, and for me entertaining is the same as a boy or a girl. It's all about giving the audience what they want. I like to become a boy after the show, to show them the transformation. Plus, it makes driving home a heck of a lot easier.

Be Strappin, Anson Reigns, and Vincent Von Dyke
Photo By: Sara Moses

Glitz Glam and Alexis Mateo
Official Drag Handbook

THE
NAKED TRUTH
Photo Credit: Kristopher Reynolds Photography
a light-hearted
advice column
Love,
Sex, &
Relationships
KristoferReynolds@SpotlightTodayMagazine.com

The Naked Truth is a light-hearted advice column on love, sex and relationships from Kristofer Reynolds. He welcomes questions on any aspect of your love life, love interests, or lack thereof. Although his opinions are certainly not the end all, his refreshing point of view, and open mind, may help you find the clarity you need in any situation

Kristofer has been with his partner for 13 years, and holds a degree in Psychology from the prestigious Rollins College. He has had a wide variety of personal experiences, both before and during his relationship, and an open mind to the variety of relationships, people and encounters we have in our quest for love and sex. Don't be afraid to ask any questions at all. Your privacy will be respected and all things kept anonymous. Look forward to hearing from you!

Curiosity in love

Dear Kristofer,

My boyfriend and I have been together a few years now and we have a great sex life, but he wants to try something new that I'm not so sure about. He wants to explore having 3 ways, and maybe even an open relationship. I just don't know how I feel about it even though the thought does make me curious. We are 21 and 22, and haven't really been with many people, but this kind of makes me feel like I am not enough for him. On the other side though, I am kind of curious about experimenting with other people, but it kind of scares me too. What should I do? -Confused

Dear Confused,

This is definitely a big decision for any relationship, and depending on your mindset and trust in one another, it could turn out great or it could be detrimental to both of you. I have seen it go both ways. To be honest, however, in successful cases the couple had a deep trust and love for one another and the casual sexual relationships they had were just that.

Some may argue you are opening doors you shouldn't, and they are entitled to their opinion, but I feel that sexual exploration is as healthy and normal as monogamy, as long as you both are on the same level about it.

Curiosity is natural, and at your respective ages with little experience outside of each other, this is not an unexpected scenario. The bottom line is this. You both must be on a level of trust and understanding that allows for you to have the mindset that no one can threaten your personal relationship together. Your relationship must be on one level, and anything else on another. If that isn't established and strong, then it just won't work. Inviting someone into your sex life is one step in itself. As long as you both are interested in that person, and they are equally interested in BOTH of you, it generally works out quite nicely, at least from my personal experience.

Maybe you should try that first and see how it works before exploring the open relationship aspect. You may find you don't need to explore a fully open relationship after all.

A letter from a Mother

I have been married to my husband for 23 years. I am 40!!! We had 3 sons. We are high school sweethearts as well. Our sons are 23, 21 and 19 years old. Two of our sons are gay. We support them 100%.

All I know is that between myself and my husband, 23 years has had a lot of give and take. We have been through what feels like so much already, and we still have so long to go. I have tried to immerse myself in the gay culture. I love Drag! I love Ru Paul! I love my sons.

I am a female heterosexual, and from my experience about love, sex, and relationships, it is all the same for everyone, We all want to be loved and accepted for who we are and what we represent. I love my husband, and if I didn't have him in my life I can only imagine what my life would have been like, and it seems like it would have been pretty dismal and boring. Thanks for listening- Lori J.

Dear Lori,

Thank you so much for sharing that story. It's beautiful and uplifting to know that we are in a time where more and more parents are embracing their gay children instead of trying to change them, or worse. Love is a strong power that we all have to use on everyone around us. I am happy for you and your husband, and I am happy for your children who are lucky enough to have parents like you. All the best to you and your family. Spread the love!

That's the Naked Truth for this edition...until next time-

Kristofer Reynolds

Please submit any questions for future articles to
KristoferReynolds@SPOTLIGHTTODAYMagazine.com

Photo: Devon James, Justice Darnell, and Jagger Blue. ,mm

Stats:
- Name: Jane E. Phee
- Parents: Daniel F. & Flora M. Phee
- Date of Birth: November 24, 1963

- Place of Birth: Rochester, NY
- Date Departed: June 9, 2011
- Cause of Death: Heart-Attack

Now, let me tell you a little something about Jane…

When I was researching this memorial to Jagger Blue, I was afraid I would be intruding on the personal life of a local icon. LET ME TELL YOU!!! Jane was so well loved by the ENTIRE community, not just for her ability to be a male illusionist, that I received many touching testimonials to her LIFE!!!

Jane's family…

Jane grew up on a suburban street in Rochester. She was an only child who had not one, but TWO sets of cousins on the same street!! They were so close; she considered them her brothers and sisters. She grew up in a loving home and had fun with Dad, but revered her mother's strength. I was told that when she was younger, Mrs. Phee had jumped into freezing cold water to save a young girl from drowning. Jane really admired her for that.

She was particularly close to one aunt whom she lovingly called "Uncle Betty." Jane never had children of her own, but LOVED kids; and they LOVED her!! It's my understanding Jane took many a youth under her wing, and several of them called her 'Mom.' She was a mentor & friend to them all. They only had to bat their eyes, or smile, and she melted (unless they were in real trouble!) One in particular, Katherine, was called Meow-Meow Kitty by Jane. Seems Jane had a knack for giving EVERYONE nicknames and used them on a VERY regular basis!!

Jane ADORED all kinds of animals and her pets were her 'kids.' You can tell by that alone, what a loving & nurturing person she was. When I asked, "Who did Jane consider her 'chosen' family?", I got a list of people she knew for decades, that included Valarie, Rosalie, Roseanne, Shelagh, Donna, Suzie, Ashley & Devon, Annie, & Kim. Again, a testament to how she had such a positive influence in people's lives!

I have to add, here, that I was told SEVERAL times, that once you met Jane, you immediately loved her because she made you feel like her best friend. She treated everyone like they were special to her. She could be whatever you needed her to be at any moment in time, like a chameleon… "Her sense of humor would leave you laughing until you cried. When you were around Jane, no matter what your troubles, life was good. You just couldn't help but feel good around Jane." Jane was one of those people who would light up a room when she arrived!! She had MANY friends who loved and supported her in everything she did!

A little background for you…

Jane was FIRST generation American, and was able to visit Scotland and connect with her parents' stories of their hometowns. Her favorite game since she was old enough to walk was soccer, and, it's my understanding, she was pretty darn good at it!

She attended Olympia High School 1977-1981 in Greece, NY. Jane excelled in MATH. She was the "go-to" girl if you needed help from basic math to calculus! She participated in dance, singing, golf, playing the trumpet, and teaching herself how to play the piano as extracurricular activities. She was also on the Soccer & Swim Teams. Jane BROKE records when she swam! Go figure, an INTELLIGENT ATHLETE!! In her teen years, she loved jazz and old Scottish Folk Tunes which she would sing with her father. According to her friends that knew her for many years, Jane was always diversified in her interests and the word "CAN'T" was NOT a word in her vocabulary!

Right after graduation, she went to school in Kissimmee, FL to become a Certified Travel Agent, and went to college to study business. The only extracurricular subject she was interested in after high school was PARTYING!! She then moved to Dallas, TX, to begin her adult life.

A little bit about her love life...

Her first love, and heartbreak, was Mike in high school. Seems he was gay, too! Did she believe in love at first sight? YES!!! She told a close friend when they were out one night, "See that woman over there? I'm going to marry her someday!" So the courtship began... I was also told that because of her outgoing personality, she UNINTENTIONALLY broke many-a-heart herself! She really did make everyone she met feel truly special.

One of the most romantic things she ever did was rent a limousine for her girlfriend's 30th birthday, complete with bar! Flowers were waiting at a friend's house as a surprise! She fretted and planned this for a while and was excited she pulled it off.

Jane's loving partner, Celeste, told me this story about "a night in the life of..." Jane allowed Celeste's two young children, Hailey (Hailey Boo or HayHay to Jane) & Mykel (Mikey, Bubby) to play 'make-up' with her one night. By the time the kids were done with Jane, she looked like the Joker from the new *Batman* with the make-up running down her face. Now I think that's pretty cool, HOWEVER, Celeste does NOT like clowns! So what does Jane do? CHASE Celeste all over the house!!! Yup, typical Jane...

"What role did she play in the house?" Seems Jane was the "10 minute cook" and could throw together a fabulous meal in no time!! The other 'chore' that Jane INSISTED on doing was cleaning the bathroom!! (Psst ~ She could have come to MY house to do that anytime she wanted!!)

How she paid the bills...

Jane's first job was at a Sandwich Shoppe in Rochester, New York.

The job she loved most was mentoring troubled youth for Pasco Sheriff's Youth Ranch & Opportunity Store. Remember what I said about kids? She felt fulfilled by this, like it was her calling. She was on cloud nine when she was promoted to Store Manager! Then she knew she was right where she belonged! But that was just her day job...

Jane was also the proud owner of Mystic Productions, her karaoke business. As I mentioned before, she used to sing with her Dad and pursued singing as an extracurricular activity in high school, so it was a perfect fit for Jane! Turns out, she was a natural performer!! "She had a great zest for life, was very energetic and loved music. She loved being on a microphone!" She was a self-starter and her own motivator. She ALWAYS accomplished whatever she put her mind to do!

When I asked, "What job did she dislike the most?" the resounding consensus was, "window tinting with Valarie!!!" Seems Jane had a knack for cutting herself... A LOT! Not only THAT, for some reason, windows would BREAK around her!!! Valarie laughed when she told me, "When I really didn't want to work, I'd call Jane to help and just KNEW the workload would get a lot lighter with her around!!"

A little more history...

Jane had plenty of nick-names (probably because she was so good at giving them!) including: Janers, Phee, JP, Phee-Phee, Pheester, Poo-Poo Head, Calamity Jane, & Karaoke Jane.

"Calamity Jane" might have come from working with Valarie, OR, from the soccer injuries to her knee, OR, from being the proverbial bull-in-a-china-shop, OR, from her bicep being ripped from her left arm after lifting a deceptively heavy box which had to be surgically repaired!! I only mention this because if you watch the memorial video of her life, that type of injury would NEVER be believed with the ENERGY she had on stage.

You know when you're sitting on the sofa with the love of your life, all snuggled up and cozy and your lover says, "I love you honey, BUT, I'd do that anytime!!"? Wanna know who Jane said that about??? Janet Jackson

What was her most rebellious moment? When getting married to Devon, she said, "I'm going on strike! No more cleaning house!!!" I also have to say that this was a real head-scratcher for her friends. Jane was very accommodating and easy-going. Her WORD was GOLD! If she committed to something, she DID it.

The one accomplishment that she was most proud of OUTSIDE of work was getting her motorcycle license. She didn't ride all that much, but it fit with something else her friends told me about her, one of her mantras, "Live every day to the fullest."

"One funny time in Jane's life was when her boss told her that Holiday, Florida must have a lot of power outages! Jane was always calling her work when she was late and told them that the reason for her being late was because her power was out and that was why her alarm did not go off, so that is why she would be late to work." ~ Devon

When I asked, "what did she like to do in her spare time?" they all agreed; watch sports (tennis, golf, & DALLAS football to be exact) & eat GOOD food!! Shelagh's Mom, Annie, made her absolute favorite home-made food, English Sausage Rolls!! She LOVED Robin's pasta fazul, even stopped by to get some to go when she knew Robin made it & couldn't sit down right then and there to enjoy it!! As a matter of fact, I'm told she did that to a lot of her friends! If there was GOOD food around, Jane was there to help enjoy it.

OK, you can tell by now that Jane was a very intelligent woman, right? As a matter-of-fact, she was called the "Jeopardy Queen" with all the info she knew. So when I threw out there, "What's the funniest thing she ever said?" I heard crickets... Seems Jane was THE jokester! She LOVED JOKES & making people laugh! So I re-worded it a little, "What's the funniest thing she ever said UNINTENTIONALLY?"

She apparently liked playing video games and she, like most of us, got frustrated with one and blurted out, "What the heck, this is rated E for EASY!" If you need this explained, you're too old to understand <chuckles>. When asked what was she really bad at, that she would have loved to be great at, video games, bowling, & softball were the answers.

JAGGER BLUE...

"(Jagger) was around Drag for many years, but took special interest in supporting the Drag Kings/MI's. A close friend to the local greats, D.C., Devon James, and Gage Gatlyn, (Jagger said he) wanted to help them show the new kings that "it takes more than wearing 'skateboard clothes, facial hair and standing on stage to be called a King. It was to be earned!" (Jagger) took all of ('himself,') put on some hot men's clothes, added some bling here, some sparkle there and headed to Talent Night at Chill Chamber in New Port Richey. Jagger's first performance was *Pour Some Sugar On Me* and shut the house DOWN! The energy and excitement Jagger brought to the stage was mind-blowing!! (He) had girls AND guys throwing money at (him)! Yes, Jagger Blue was born!" So says Robin (the pasta fazul maker) & D.C.'s wife.

The name "Jagger Blue" was created by a combination of Jagger's fondness for Yager Bomb shots (but changed it to Jagger) and his fur-kid, Blue.

"Jagger became a drag king after 4 years of dressing and helping me. (He) wanted to show all kings, new as well as old, that there should be no reason why they couldn't look their best, and perform their best, no matter what their status as a performer was." ~ Devon

You might have guessed both his most memorable performance and signature song was *Pour Some Sugar On Me*. True to form, his preferred genre was Classic Rock, however, he was known to mix it up. He called the 'Chill Chamber' in New Port Richey, FL his home bar since MOST of his performances were there. EVERYONE at the bar loved him so much, that they re-named 'Yager Bomb' to 'Jagger Blue!. His signature costumes were blue (duh!) and had BLING. Jagger would walk on stage in a wonderful suit and by the time the number was over, he would only be half-dressed!! He had a habit of shedding his clothes with a LOT of high energy and the fans LOVED him for it!

Jagger hit the stage for the first time on September 17, 2010 and was only able to entertain for 8 months before his passing, BUT, in those 8 months, Jagger Blue made such an impact on everyone who saw him, he was known by many, loved by most, and missed by all!

Tidbits...

- "If you don't want an honest answer, don't ask the question!"
- Purchasing her own home was an important high-light in her life.
- She knew where she stood with God. "He lives inside us. I don't need a church to tell me that."
- Jagger absolutely HATED feet, PERIOD; hers and anyone else.
- The night the Challenger exploded (January 28, 1986) she mourned the lives of those on board at the ABC Lounge with friends. It was a shock to us all.
- The fall of the Berlin Wall (November 9, 1989). Loved the fact that it came down and hoped it would bring rights and unity to the region.
- Gulf War (August 2, 1990 – February 28, 1991). Bush waited too long, back in the day, we would have stuck a flag in it and called it ours!!
- Earthquake in Haiti (January 12, 2010). Happy that so many entertainers came together again to aid a devastated area with little or no resources of their own.

What others said...

- *Jane's heart was as big as the sun and just as warm too!*
- *Jane was the most kind, forgiving, loving, and fun person another could ever meet. She would literally give you the shirt off her back whether she knew you or not!*
- *She was truly a great spirited person. She will be missed by many and will always be loved by all of the people that she has touched in her life.*
- *She loved the girls from the Safety Harbor Ranch and listened to their dreams and goals for their lives with real interest. ...She is and will always be greatly missed by all who knew her, worked with her, and she will forever be in our memories of a life cut so very short. May God bless her and the legacy she left us all.*

➢ *Jane was a beautiful person and touched the lives of so many people...*

➢ *Pheester you will truly be missed. I have had the pleasure to be your friend for over 20 years and have great memories. You have always been there for me and I will never forget you. Thank you for being YOU and a great friend.*

➢ *To ANYONE who knew Jane, her presence will be missed tremendously. Her free spirit, contagious laugh, caring heart, & beautiful smile are all things we have to hold onto for we were BLESSED to know her and be called her friend.*

➢ *Along with the long list of lifetime friends, she had an impact on each and every one of us. You touched us all Jane and you are deeply missed. Thank you for being the amazing person/friend you were.*

➢ *Friends where lucky enough to be touched by her in many ways. Her smile... Her chuckle... Her voice... will never be forgotten.*

➢ *Jane was one in a million and I am honored to have called her "friend" She will be dearly missed and the times we shared will never be forgotten.*

➢ *To know Jane, was to love Jane. She never met a stranger. She had a positive impact on so many lives. I had the honor to know Jane for the past 12 years, both socially and professionally... her hearty laugh, great smile, and incredible sense of humor will be greatly missed.*

➢ *Such an amazing person such as Jane. She will be missed by all of us. To her parents, thank you for such a wonderful human being,*

➢ *Jane was one of my greatest childhood friends - we were on the same swim team for 5 years - we spent many, many hours together - our families shared many wonderful memories. Jane will be missed...*

➢ *Nobody had a bigger heart or a heartier laugh than Janie. I will never forget the wonderful childhood memories of time spent with Jane in Rochester. She always made time for you, no matter how busy she was, and every time you spoke with her, you walked away with a smile on your face. She never failed to brighten my day. She was quite simply ...one in a million! XOX*

➢ *I have known her for about 6 years now and Jane was more than just a friend; she was an amazing person. She was always so kind and considerate to everyone she knew and we always welcomed seeing her at every opportunity. Her passing will not only leave a void in our lives, but in the hearts of everyone who knew her. Jane's memory will always remain deep within my heart.*

- *Jane was a beautiful light in my life for several years and I treasure the time I knew her. She had one of the kindest souls a person can have.*
- *Jane was loved by so many and her loss will leave a permanent impact on all the lives she touched.*
- *I only knew for a short time, but the time I did know her she was a very kind and warm person.*
- *Jane you are missed so much. The kids talk about you each day, they look up at the sky to talk with you, 'cause they understand Angels go to heaven, it is hard to go by the house, and you are not there to serve my coffee :-). You are LOVED... and MISSED so much.*
- *We will cherish the memories of her during the good old days back on Blue Grass Lane.*
- *She was loved and respected by all who knew her.*

I don't know about you, but I'm disappointed I never had the privilege of meeting Jane or watching Jagger perform live. He is a King I admire for "putting it all on the stage" and caring about the future of male illusionist performers. I tip my hat to you, sir.

Maxi Pad and Charles Horner with Todd Kachinski-Kottmeier,
and Afeelya Bunz
Official Drag Handbook

CONFIDENCE
"To succeed in life, you need two things: ignorance and confidence." Mark Twain
Kevin Reed
@Spotlight Magazine.com

Happy Spring To Everyone!

The birds are building nests; the butterflies who were once drab colored caterpillars are colorfully displaying their wings. Newborns are plentiful, and humans are ritualistically "Spring cleaning" their homes as they prepare for change! This is indeed a time of renewal; physical, emotional, and spiritual renewal!

As I think of this wondrous time of the year, I encourage all readers to embrace positive change, especially with respect to self-image and self-confidence.

Over the years, I have been fortunate to work in a Public Health capacity, and a lot of my work has been in the LGBT community, either behind a microscope, in health clinics, or conducting community level health surveillance. One of the common themes that I have seen during my work has been what appears to be an epidemic of low self-esteem and lack of self-love in the LGBT community! While many of us have overcome our insecurities with time, faith, and counseling, a great number of our brothers and sisters are still dealing with issues of negative self-image, especially issues related to body image and outer beauty.

With this in mind, and the theme of spring, rebirth, and renewal, I encourage us all to move forward in our lives with positive self-images, and to strengthen ourselves daily with love and affirmation. I read, pray or meditate daily. I find that doing so, is a wonderful ritual to set the tone for my day. I often say to others, and myself "I love you," "I love me," "You are beautiful, "I am beautiful" etc. The power that comes from such positive statements of love and affirmation are amazing, and grow metastatically in communities! Affirmations are among the building blocks of CONFIDENCE and healthy self-image, and are vital to ourselves as members of the LGBT community, as well as members of the human race at large!

Go forward and love yourself! Be confident with "who" and "what" you are on the outside, and remember that TRUE love and beauty emanate from the inside! Do not be afraid to express love or beauty outwardly through self-expression or in words to others! "Carpe diem" ("seize the day" in Latin) and do so with confidence and self-assurance! We are ALL worthy of being true to ourselves, loving ourselves, and nurturing the self-image that we feel in our hearts and visualize in our minds!

Happy Spring!
Kevin B. Reed, MPH

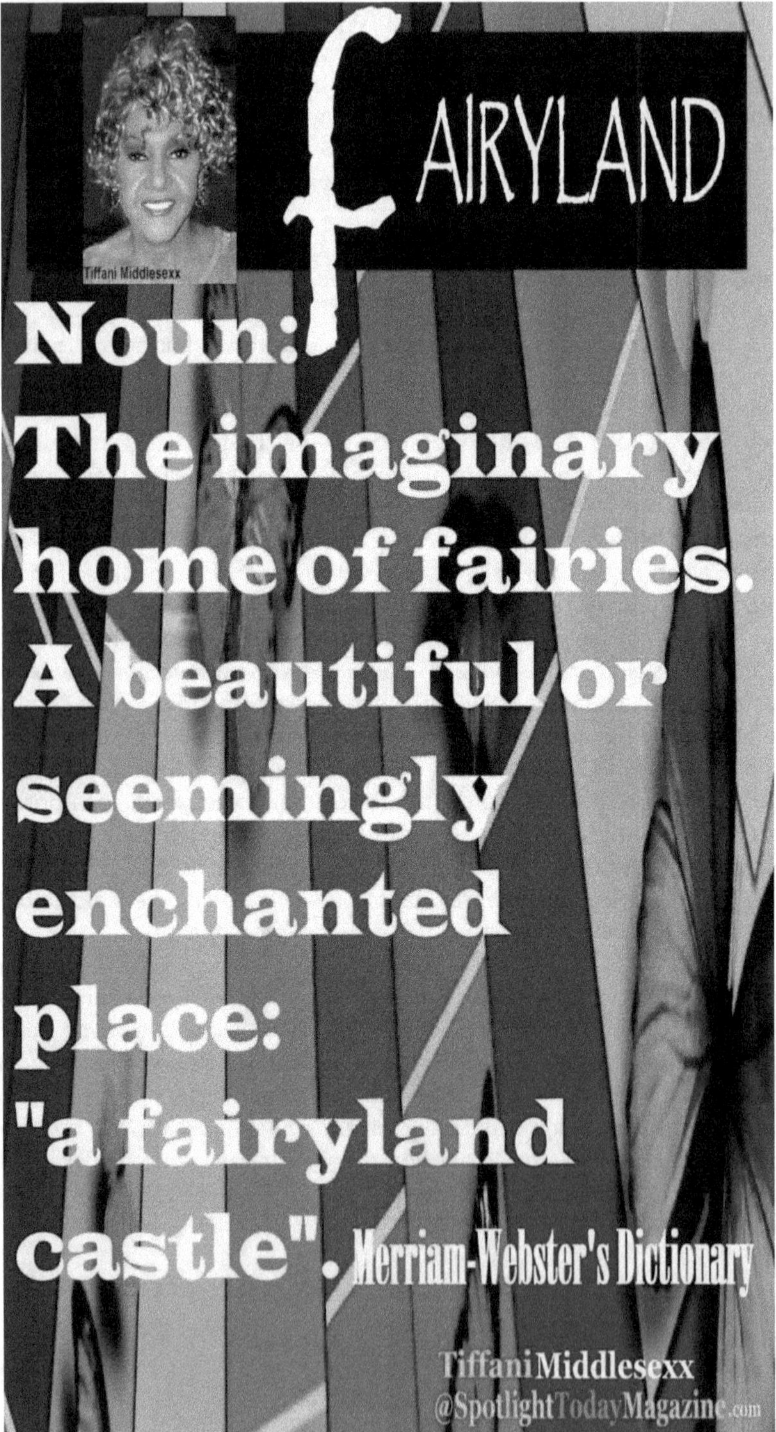
Tiffani Middlesexx
fAIRYLAND
Noun: The imaginary home of fairies. A beautiful or seemingly enchanted place: "a fairyland castle". Merriam-Webster's Dictionary
Tiffani Middlesexx
@SpotlightTodayMagazine.com

Hello everyone out there in Fairyland.

My name is Tiffani T. Middlesexx and I have been asked to write a column about my experiences from my early days in drag.

Where should I start? Well I started doing drag at the age of 15, when I would sneak out my bedroom window, climb down the drainage pipe, and run over to my friend's apartment to get in makeup. I was not known as Tiffani; that came later. I was Geraldine Lamarr Starr. At fifteen, I already thought I knew everything about drag. BOY WAS I WRONG! For the sake of time, let us skip ahead a couple years to my 17th birthday.

This is when I secretly landed my first job in a drag show. I was still in high school, but the bar owner did not seem to care, he loved my act and I worked cheap.

Things were very different back then. The drinking age was eighteen, with the Viet Nam war fracturing the country. It was a crazy time, but enough of that bullshit, back to drag. I remember, if you were in drag, you had to have at least two pieces of male attire visible on what you were wearing. Have you ever heard of something so ridiculous?

My good friend Bobby Bruno (AKA Jennifer Foxx) was arrested under this statute, and was not even in drag at the time. He was sporting a beard and mustache, and they arrested Bobby for being in drag. I mean hell, he had a beard and mustache for God's sake!

What were you thinking, that the bearded lady had escaped from the circus?

Well, that is it for now there will be more to follow in my series... "DRAG, THE GOOD OLD, OLD SCHOOL DAYS!"

TotiYanah Diamond and Patricia Grand
Official Drag Handbook

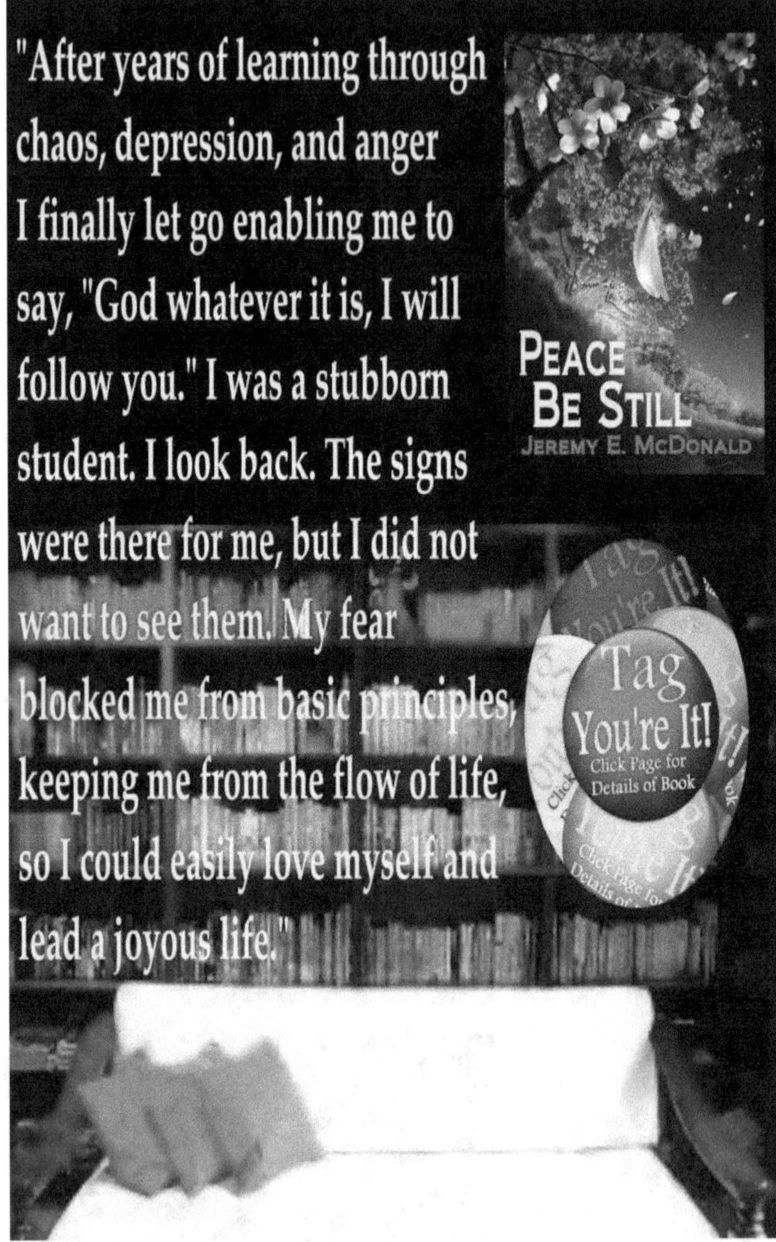

Peace Be Still by Jeremy E. McDonald

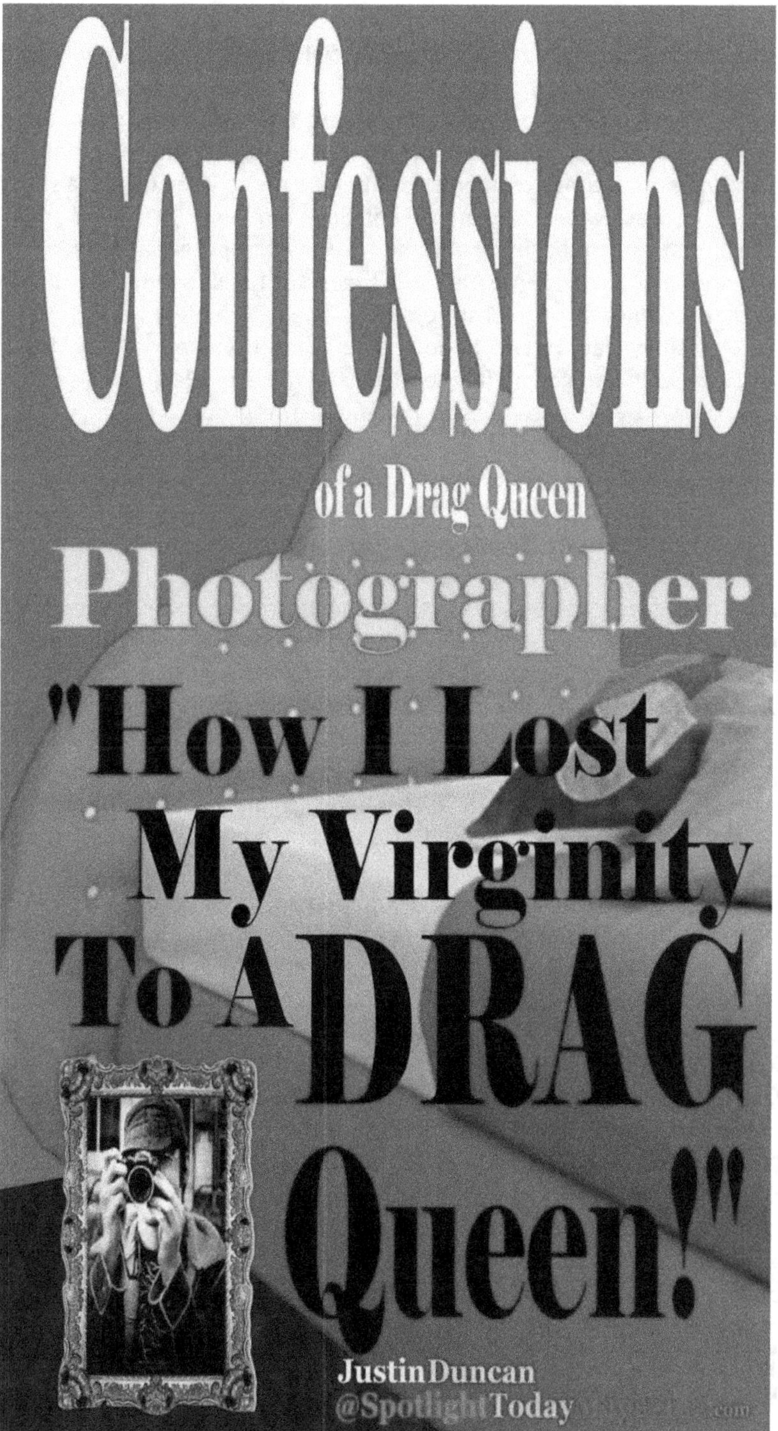
Confessions
of a Drag Queen
Photographer
"How I Lost
My Virginity
To A DRAG
Queen!"
Justin Duncan
@SpotlightToday

I was eighteen. Eighteen seems so grown up looking at some of the gay boys today, but I still felt like a child at the time. I cannot say I cared much about anything back then though. I sure as hell didn't care about staying at someone else's place. And yes, I was having fun, but it was a kick of anorexia that gave me my "barely legal" twink boy look, and an undermined case of depression that led me to just not give a shit.

It was when I started hanging out with a friend named Ashley...that I started coming into my true gay boy potential. Looking back on it, she may have been a bad influence...but I still love her to this day. She changed my life in the best possible way.

Ashley had sort of adopted me when I was a lost boy. I didn't dress very well, had god awful mop-top, and my eyes were always covered by my hair if by chance I wasn't looking at the ground. Ashley's parents owned a successful business, and her parents were very generous. She had her own beautiful house and drove a black Mustang. She changed me.

She bought me new clothes, she styled and dyed my hair, taught me how to "accessorize", and even taught me how to drink. She wasn't a fag-hag at all...She was a Fag-Creator...a Gay-Saver. After she was satisfied with my new look, she was ready to let me loose in the world. She took me to my first gay bar in St. Petersburg. It was called GCS at the time, and has since been renamed. I remember how nervous I was when I realized it had a 21+ sign on the door...but it seemed to not exist when I walked up. It was like gay magic.

That night I got more drunk than I had ever and still have ever been. My first shot ever was a jager-bomb...I think I had 7. After that came my first taste of a Long Island Iced Tea, followed by many other drinks. I cannot remember if it was Ashley buying the drinks, or the entire bar, but I finally learned how easy it was to talk to people. I was an anti-social kind of kid, but finally learned it's not so hard to talk to absolutely everyone when you're so drunk, and they're so friendly. I'm sure it had nothing to do with my ripped jeans, muscle shirt, or the fact that I was drunk of my ass and couldn't stand. I loved that bar. After having a water bottle dumped in my face on a regular basis, I think that's about the time we would usually leave. We came back several times. That's where I met him. He was tall, dark, and beautiful. And he was nice.

I was standing outside the bar while Ashley smoked a cigarette and told me how cute I looked. Even to this day, all compliments are taken lightly...but it's not by purpose, it's by prone. It is hard to believe someone telling you you are beautiful when you have spent so much time thinking you're not. So, as my first lover walked up the sidewalk to enter the gay bar in frustration Ashley shouted to the beautiful Puerto Rican boy, "TELL HIM HE LOOKS GOOD!", and as he opened the door to the bar he looked me up and down and smiled to say, "You're Adorable..."

Inside the bar, we exchanged eye contact several times while Ashley nudged me to go talk to him. "He already said you were adorable, he thinks you're cute! Go talk to him!" As nervous as I was, I think it was obvious that I was not getting up from the bar stool for the rest of the night unless it was to leave. Finally, it was she that went up to him and dragged him to come sit next to us. That is when he told us he was a drag queen performer. I asked him, "What kind?" Knowing better now, I would not have had to ask but looking back at how naïve and oblivious I was, it must have been really, really adorable.

I looked at the photo of him from inside his wallet for a good minute and a half, still wondering why he was showing me a photo of his mother, and finally he laughed so hard I became embarrassed. I handed him back the photo and looked down as if I had done something wrong. He held it back up to show me again, "That's ME!!!"

He shook his hand in front of me as it would better boggle my mind into understanding, "That's me! Me as a girl...I dress in Drag!" Finally, it clicked, and I knew why everyone was laughing so hard.

When the night before finally came, after we exchanged phone calls for about a month, he came over to Ashley's for a party. That night it seemed odd to me why Ashley had fallen asleep on the sofa. He needed a ride home and I did not want to wake her, but she had already pulled out the sofa-bed for herself. Though I was a bit confused as to why she would have not told me she wanted to sleep on the couch, the boy chimed in with a excitedly reassuring voice, "WELL, looks like I'm staying here!" So we laid down; we kissed, we cuddled.

The day after we spent driving around with Ashley, having fun, and holding hands, IN PUBLIC. I had never done that. That night he showed me videos of him performing and I could not believe how good he was at it. I remember feeling how impressed I was, how much work he must have had to do, and how much fun he was having. He had even showed me a few dance moves and put on a small performance for me to some of the songs he loved performing. We had driven by his house so he could pick up some of his stuff, but dressing in drag was not one of the things he was able to show me that night. Instead, he wanted to watch a movie. Once again, Ashley had fallen asleep on the sofa bed, but I was okay with it this time. She had a DVD player in her room. The movie was still on when we woke up the next morning. We never got past the menu screen.

First times are always hard. At least, I've never heard of a first time when a virgin just hopped on. I have heard some painful stories, but this wasn't even like that. It didn't hurt at all. In fact, it was fantastic for what it was, a first time. I don't regret it at all. What I do regret, was how I reacted the night after, the night he dressed in drag for me. The night I met her...

I wasn't ready. Seeing her in photos, and seeing her perform on video, are just two different worlds when faced with reality. I wasn't exactly comfortable with the idea, but I was more excited like a kid than I should have been. I was still naïve. I was still thinking that it was sort of all just a performance. But it became real…and I reacted in the worst kind of way. She explained to me that she was afraid of this happening, and said that it's happened before, and that it's a risk she always has to take…but she hopes that one day someone would be okay with it. She was hoping that someone would be me. I didn't hear any of it. I asked her to leave. I called Ashley and asked her to help me come up with a reason so he, or she, didn't have to, or couldn't be here anymore. I did the worst possible thing and to this day, I am sorry. I am so sorry.

Years later, he recognized me at a tea dance in south St. Petersburg. He was still performing, and I was still caught in a world of boy trouble. We talked for about an hour, and I finally got to say how sorry I was for reacting the way I did, but all he said was that it was okay. What else can you say. I got to apologize and that much made me feel worlds better. Even now, I can remember how badly I wanted to say I'm sorry and I'm happy I had my chance. I had expected, or maybe even wanted, for him to tell me how awful I was…but he didn't. He invited me to see his show. I had never gotten to see him perform…this was my chance to make it up to him. This was my chance to see him perform…I didn't get that chance.

As fate would have it, I was not able to stay and watch. I had a very jealous and very chaining relationship at the time. When my boyfriend saw us talking, he became jealous. The guy I was with dragged me away and forced me to leave, or be ditched. I should have stayed… I didn't get a chance to tell him we were leaving. As this was just one bad relationship amongst the rest of the lot that were just like it. The only way I feel I'll ever be happy is to announce that I am single indefinitely. Maybe this will help me stop hurting myself and others. I have never had ONE good relationship that I can look back on say I was happy in. To this day…I've still never gotten to see him perform…I've never gotten to see her perform. But I am still hoping to this day, that one day,… I might.

Ryan Royale and Vivikah Kayson
Official Drag Handbook

So, you want
to be a
Drag
Queen
Photo Credit:
Big Mike
Candi Samples
@SpotlightTodayMagazine.com

Last week I was asked, "How to jump start a career in the Drag Queen industry."

After putting much thought into it, I realized that was not easy to answer because this business is like no other. However, if you are creative enough, and believe in yourself.

You must create a bigger persona. Don't be a clone. Be original. Your first step is making sure that what you are aiming for is what you really want. Standing out in a crowd can be a double edged sword!

So you want to be a Drag Queen?

Okay, Gypsy Rose Lee once said, "You got to get a gimmick if you want to get a hand." Some of you ask, 'Who is Gypsy Rose Lee' and to that I say she was doing Burlesque before Cher was. Remember; be original with getting a gimmick. What type of drag queen do you want to be? Be decisive in what you do because there are excessively many other queens out there that will jump at a chance to steal your chance to perform; go after what you really want and start now.

Once you have a specific vision of what you want to do, get started. Here are a few ways to start. Get a job at one of the local bars or clubs, one that has a drag show. Becoming a local favorite even before you start performing in the show helps build a fan base. There is nothing better than having a loving and supportive fan base. Volunteer to perform in a benefit show, even major celebrities give back. Compete in a local pageant or contest.

Get your name out there, meet some of the other girls in shows, or just put yourself in your local Pride parade. It will surprise you how well you can do when you believe in yourself and enjoy what you are doing. Whenever you are performing be genuine, it will come across to the crowd. The crowd loves someone they can support and find special and worthy of looking up to.

Lastly, give yourself time to accomplish your goal. Be patient with yourself, be realistic, work hard and don't forget to enjoy what you are doing. Always remember you can be unmade as quickly as you were made, just like a bed. Another legend once said " It's better to be looked at than overlooked" Her name was Mae West and if anyone knew how to create a big persona, she was one of the best.

Till we meet again on the pages of Spotlight

Hugs Candi Kisses XOXO

Naomi Wynters and Adora (with Todd Kachinski-Kottmeier)
Official Drag Handbook

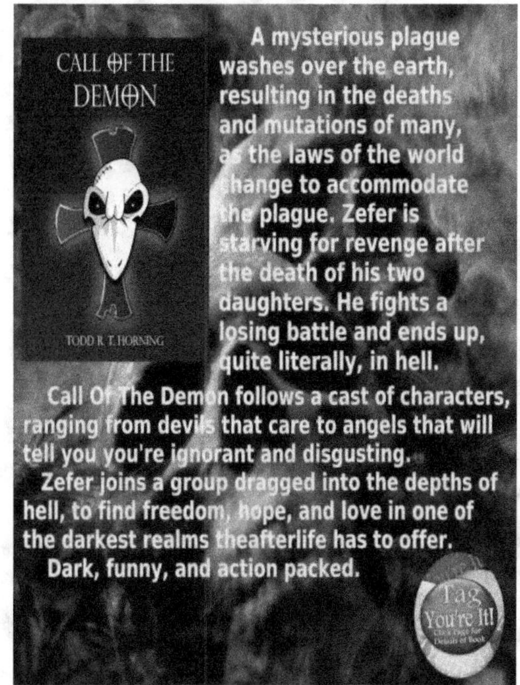

Call of the Demon by Todd R.T. Horning

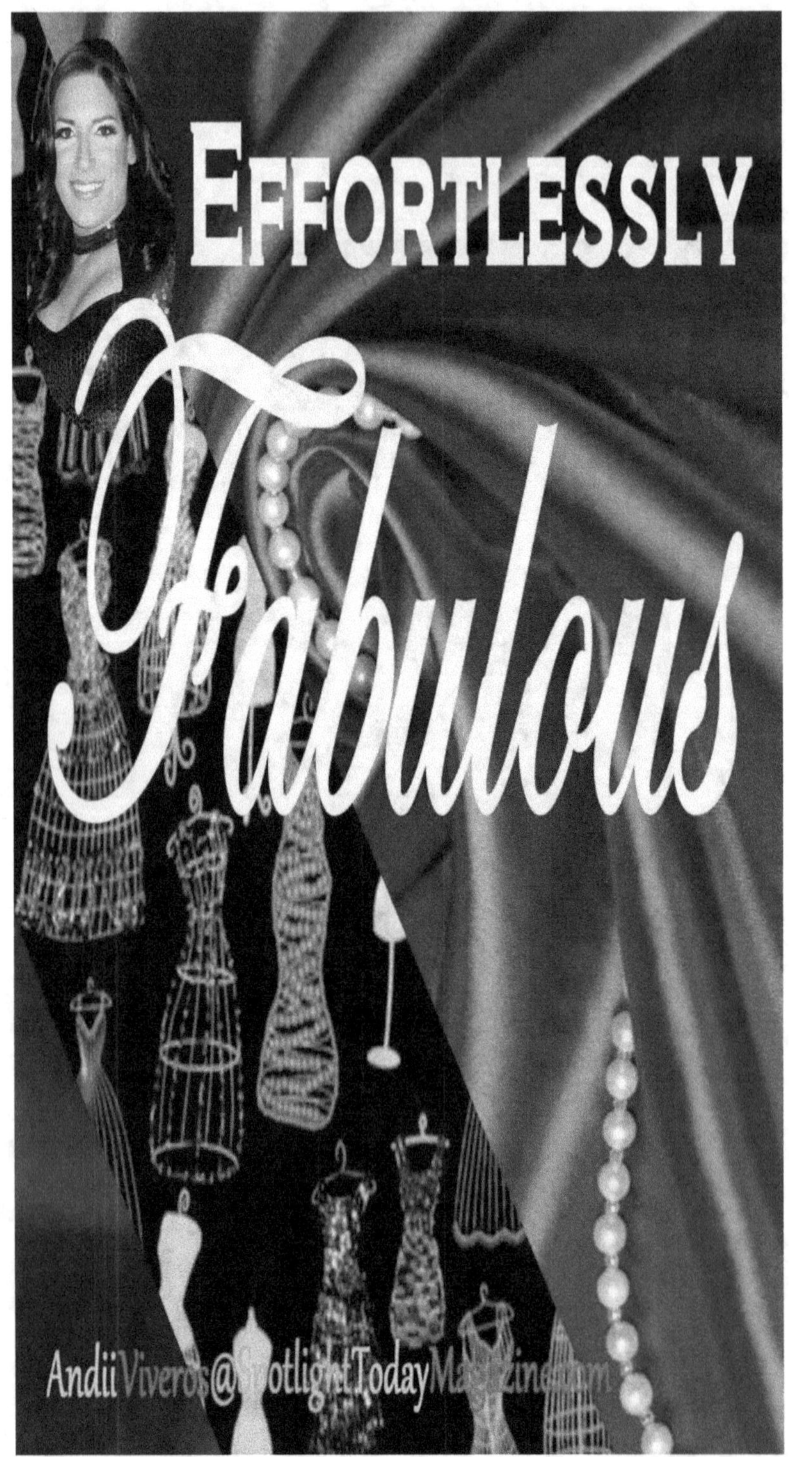

EFFORTLESSLY
Fabulous
AndiiViveros@SpotlightTodayMagazine.com

Spring is in full bloom and this season's most demanded trends are yours for the taking! For you ladies, a blast from the past is very popular for spring- the Polka-Dot pencil skirt. Dressed up or down, you can easily turn this from office chic, paired with a crisp white blouse- to shopping with the girls, playing well together with a classic white tank top and pastel cardigan. Give off the look of maturity, while still bringing youthfulness and sexiness to the table with this outfit!

SKIRT- $40 Alfani, *Macy's* **BLACK PUMPS- $29** Nine West
Flower Ring- $8 dots.com

Become instantly pulled together with this dazzling crystal embellished ring.
Fireball Hoop Earrings- $7 dots.com

Feel like a South Beach socialite with these earrings inspired by the television hit, *Basketball Wives.*

LONG-SLEEVED SHIRT IN NAVY/WHITE-$29, PRINTED SHORTS-$29, Target Stores

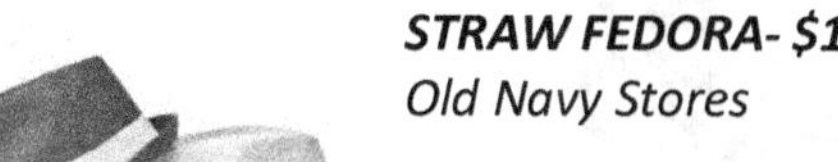

STRAW FEDORA- $15
Old Navy Stores

Pair your fabulous outfit with these fedora hats to instantly spice things up with carefree island flair.

WOVEN BELT- $19
American Eagle Outfitters

Add an instant pop of color to your ensemble with this printed belt.

I hope you gentlemen are ready for the
un-filled days of spring and summer that
are nearly upon us. Those long days of
finishing work then meeting friends for a
nk at the local spot or gathering with the
ommunity at your local pride celebration
rapidly approaching! In order for you to
have the best time possible, you have to
feel and look your best- and what better
way to do that than this season's hottest
designs at fraction of the price? Look no
ther than your local Target store! Luxury
hion company, *The Webster*, specializing
in high end tropical and exotic menswear
will be extending their brand into stores Nationwide in early May.
This season, nothing is more comfortable than a casual pair of
printed shorts and a rolled-up, long sleeved, partially unbuttoned shirt.
Seriously- who can resist a man with a little chest showing? Throw in some
accessories such as a hat from Old Navy or a belt from American eagle
outfitters, and you will be ready to hit the town! This look is so versatile
that it can easily be taken from a beach outfit to casual brunch attire,
leaving many wondering how you pull together so well!

Birthstones for the calendar month of June

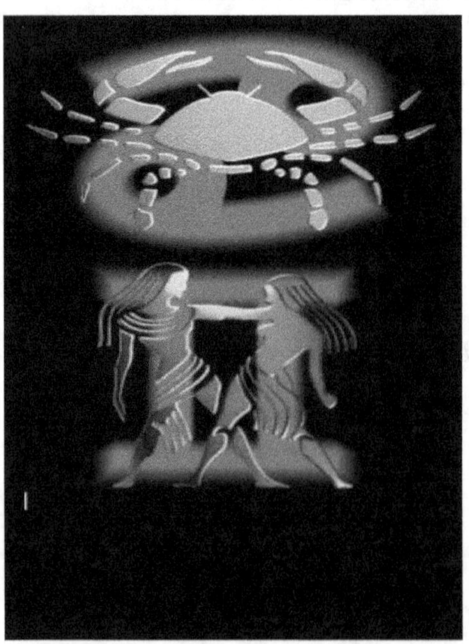

Pearl,
moonstone,
alexandrite,
agate,
chalcedony,
and emerald.
The Zodiac Signs
of Gemini and Cancer
include six additional stones:
Chrysoprase,
tiger's eye,
white sapphire,
ruby, sapphire,
and citrine.

"I'm a supporter of gay rights. And not a closet supporter either. From the time I was a kid, I have never been able to understand attacks upon the gay community. There are so many qualities that make up a human being... by the time I get through with all the things that I really admire about people, what they do with their private parts is probably so low on the list that it is irrelevant."

Paul Newman

Laws and Legislation Taking Root Around The World

Welcoming to this amazing publication. This column focuses on legislative and legal news affecting LGBTQ communities. The information is published using state and federal legislative publications, transcripts of legislative debates and hearings, public records, and court documents. Write me to help me, help other stay informed.

Anchorage, Alaska

Proposition 5, which would have added sexual orientation and transgender identity to the city's civil rights ordinance failed. Both sides of the issue attribute the outcome to a much larger than expected voter turnout.

Olympia, Washington

Same gender marriage statute signed in to law. This new law takes effect June 7, 2012. This makes Washington the seventh state to legalize same gender couples to marry. The District of Columbia also allows same gender marriages.

Washington, DC

President Obama decided not to sign an Executive Order that would have prohibited federal contractors from discriminating based on sexual orientation or gender identity.

Wayne, Ohio

Lambda Legal filed suit against Wayne Local School District on behalf of a Waynesville high school student, Maverick Couch, according to a press release. Last April, on the National Day of Silence, Couch wore a T-shirt to school that featured a rainbow sign of the fish along with the words "Jesus is not a homophobe"—and the principal ordered him to turn the shirt inside out. After more rejected requests from the school, Couch contacted Lambda Legal, who sent a letter to the school and followed with a lawsuit seeking to stop the school from prohibiting the shirt. The school will now allow Couch to wear the shirt on the National Day of Silence only.

Wilton Manors, Florida

The Securities and Exchange Commission (SEC) is claiming that George Elia, 67, used "affinity fraud" to trick gay investors in an $11-million Ponzi scheme, Courthouse News Service reported. The 19-page complaint says that "Elia's scheme was, in part, an affinity fraud: a number of the investors were members of the gay community in Wilton Manors, Florida." The SEC is suing Elia and his company as well as 212 Entertainment Club and Elia Realty as relief defendants.

Boise, Idaho

Senate State Affairs Committee shot down a proposed bill adding workplace and housing discrimination protections for GLBT individuals to Idaho's Human Rights Act.

Concord, New Hampshire

The State House voted to kill a measure that would have repealed the state's two-year-old gay marriage law. Supporters of the measure have vowed to bring it up in the next legislative session.

Reno, Nevada

Lambda Legal Defense and Education Fund filed suit on behalf of eight same gender couples. The suit seeks marriage equality for the plaintiffs. This suit challenges a constitutional amendment to the state constitution prohibiting same gender couples marrying in Nevada.

June Trivia

The Rose is the flower of June. The rose has symbolic root in many legends and poems throughout time. In one Roman legend, an angered goddess transforms a beautiful woman into a rose. Many men who wanted to win her love and hand in marriage chased the beautiful Rodanthe. Her beauty and her indecisiveness overcame men. They broke down the door to her home in pursuit of her. Diane, a goddess angered by their actions. She transformed Rodanthe into a rose and her suitors into the rose's thorns. Like this legend, many poems represent love as a rose and the rose's thorns as obstacles overcame, or to be overcome, in love.

Lipstick
And Paint
Makes a man
What he ain't...
Issue One
"How tight is your mug?"
Spring 2012
Blair Michaels
@SpotlightTodayMagazine.com

"How Tight is Your Mug?"

Let me welcome you to the first volume of my column!

I would like to thank SPOTLIGHT TODAY Magazine for giving me the opportunity to spread the word on all things about make-Up.

For me, the first thing I feel is most important is to create a great foundation, that is your mug, better known as your skin. If you do not have fabulous and flawless skin to work with, your make-up isn't going to last as long as you'd like it to. So, before you put that panstick, or cream foundation on, you need to get that mug ready! Begin with cleansing your face at least 1 hour before you apply any make-up. I love to start my routine with a facial scrub or wash. I use the Neutrogena foaming cleanser. I cannot think of a more relaxing and lovely moment, than putting on a "Queen Helena" mask. It is a thick green cream that spreads easily, and it lets you know when your mug is ready to be rinsed because it dries and cracks and you look like a zoo-loo warrior!

A great facial mask can do wonders for your skin. Depending on your skin *type*; a great mask can remove excess oils or hydrate very dry skin. Not only does this help tighten those pores, it also pulls out these annoying blackheads and really sucks your face *tight*!

Finish off with a lotion that isn't greasy, otherwise your foundation slides and you'll forever be powdering for the rest of the night. No one wants to do that for sure! Now that you have your "mug tight" you are ready to get stamped! In the next column we'll discuss the best foundations for you and your *"Tight Mug"*.

Until next time America...

Love, Lashes & Lipgloss,
Blair Michaels

**This is only a copy of the actual Magazine created in 2012.
Except for DRAG411.com, all email addresses and links
are no longer active or available.**

End of Spotlight Today, Book 7 of 10 Books

Ten Black Books

Book 1   DRAG411's
"DRAG Bully, A Survivor's Guide"

The Largest Bullying Project in LGBT History for Struggling Entertainers. Advice from over a hundred male, female, and androgynous impersonators around the world to help entertainers struggling with their family, peers, relationships, neighbors, regular jobs, venues, and successfully overcoming self-doubt. Best Selling author Todd Kachinski Kottmeier created DRAG411 to document the lives of male, female, and androgynous impersonator years ago. It is now the largest organization for impersonators on earth with over 7,000 entertainers in 32 countries. DRAG411 also operates The International Original, Official DRAG Memorial with almost a thousand names (2018). This is his 25th book, 20th World Record, and 12th book on this subject. Thousands of invitations to contribute were send out. This book contains the best of their responses, in their own words, to you.

Book 2 DRAG411's
"Original DRAG Handbook"

Over 155 female impersonators (and 1 male impersonator) from around the world share over a thousand insightful comments in the first handbook created of this art form.

Commentary shared with Todd Kachinski Kottmeier included the following contributors of The Original, DRAG Handbook to include Ada Buffet, Adora , Adrian Leigh, Afeelya Bunz, Alisa Summers, Alanna Divine, Alexis De La Mer, Alexis Mateo, Alex Serpa, Allure, Amanda Bone, Amanda Love, Amy DeMilo, Anastaia Fallon, Astasnaia Rexia, Angel gLamar, Angela Dodd, Anita Cox, April Fresh, Ashleigh Cooley, Aurora Sexton, Babette Schwartz, Bailey St. James, Barbra Herr, Barbra Seville, Beverly LaSalle, BJ Stephens, Blair Michaels, Brandon M. Caten, Brianna Lee, Brittany Moore, Brookyln Bisette, Bukkake Blaque London St. James, Cartier Paris, Cathy Craig, Champagne T. Bordeaux, Cherry Darling, Christina Paris, CoCo LaBelle, CoCo Montrese, CoCo St. James, Conundrum, Crystal Belle, Daniel Murphy, Danika Fierce, Daphne Ferraro, Dasha Nicole, Dee Gregory, Deva DaVyne, Diamond Dunhill, Diedra Windsor Walker, Dmentia Divinyl/Eva LaDeva, Echo Dazz, Esme Russell, Estelle Rivers, Eunyce Raye, Felica Fox, Felina Cashmere, Geraldine Queen Cabaret, Ginger Minj, Glitz Glam, Gilda Golden, Horchata, Ima Twat, Ineeda Twat, Jade Daniels, Jade Jolie, Jade Shanell, Jade Sotomayo, Jaeda Fuentes, Jami Micheals, Jay Santana, Jeffrey Powell, Jenna Chambers Tisdale, Jessica Jade, Jocelyn Summers, Jodie Holliday, Joey Brooks, Joshua Myers, J.P. Patrick, Juwanna Jackson, Kamden Wells, Katrina Starr, Kenny Braverman, Khrystal Leight, Kier Sarkesian, Kiki LaFlare Santangilo, Kitty D'Meaner, Kori Stevens, Krystal Amore Adonis, Lacey Lynn Taylors, Lady Clover Honey, Lady Sabrina, Lady TaJma Hall, Lakeisha Pryce, LeeAnna Love, Leigh Shannon, Lisa Carr, Lola Honey, Madisyn De La Mer, Makayla Rose Devine, Maxine Padlock (Maxi Pad), Melissa Morgan, Melody

Mayheim, Michael Wilson, Mike Astermon-Glidden, Mis Sadistic, Miss Conception, Miss Gigi, Mr. Kenneth Blake, Misty Eyez, Monique Michaels, Myah Monroe, Mystique Summers, Nairobi V. D'Viante, Naomi D-Lish, Naomi Wynters, Nicole Paige Brooks, Nikki Dynamite, Nova Starr, Ororo, Patrica Grand, Patricia Knight, Patrica Mason, Pandora DeStrange, Penelope Reigns, Polly FunkChanel, Phiore Star Liemont, Purrzsa Kyttyn, Pussy LeHoot, Raquel Payne, Rhyana Vorhman, Rickie Lee, Rusti Fawcett, Scarlett Fever, Selina Kyle, Shae Shae LaReese, Shealita Babay, Shugah Caine, Stephanie Roberts, Stephanie Stuart, Stormy Vain, Summer Breeze, Sybil Storm, Tabatha Lovall, Tatum Michelle, Teri Courtney, Tiffani Middlesexx, Timm McBride, Toni Davyne, TotiYanah Diamond,Trixie LaRue, Trixie Pleasures, Vegas Platinum, Venus D Lite, Vivika D'Angelo, Wendel Duppert and Wendy G. Kennedy.

Book 3:   DRAG411's
"Crown Me! Winning Pageants"

Hundreds of invitations sent to the titleholders, pageant promoters, judges, and talent show hosts to share their insight on not only winning pageants and contests but also owning the stage every time they perform. Their topics included auxiliary steps to success needed for song selection, dancing, movement on stage, props, backup dancers, creating your own edge, personal interviews, steps to success for winning the talent category every time you step on stage, on stage questions, eveningwear, and creative costuming. They discussed in their own unedited words, wardrobe changes, makeup, hair, shoes, when is the time to compete, qualities needed for a judge, and the top misconceptions of contestants competing in the pageantry systems.

Commentary shared with Todd Kachinski Kottmeier included the following contributors of Crown Me! to include AJ Menendez, Amy Demilo, Anastacia Dupree, Anson Reign, Bob Taylor, Breonna Tenae, Brittany T Moore, Coco Montrese, Dana Douglas, Darryl Kent, Denise Russell, Dey Jzah Opulent, Freddy Prinze Charming, Gage Gatlyn, Jay Santana , Jayden Knight, Jennifer Foxx, Joey Jay, Kori Stevens, Mis Sadistic, Mykul Jay Valentine, Natasha Richards, Rico Taylor, Sam Hare, Stephanie Stuart, Taina T. Norell, Tiffani Middlesexx, Tori Taylor, Ty Nolan, Vinnie Marconi, and Vivika D'Angelo.

Book 4:   DRAG411's
"DRAG King Guide"

Over 155 male impersonators around the world share over a thousand insightful comments in forty-one chapters.

Commentary shared with Todd Kachinski Kottmeier included the following contributors of The Official DRAG King and Male Impersonators Guide to include Aaron Phoenix, Abs Hart, Adam All, Adam DoEve, AJ Menendez, Alec Allnight, Alexander Cameron, Alik Muf, Andrew Citino, Anjie Swidergal, Anson Reign, Ashton The Adorable Lover, Atown, Ayden Layne, B J Armani, B J Bottoms, Bailey Saint James, Ben Doverr, Ben Eaten, Bootzy Edwards Collynz, Brandon KC Young-Taylor, Bruno Diaz, Cage Masters, Campbell Reid Andrews, Chance Wise, Chandler J Hart, Chasin Love, Cherry Tyler

Manhattan, Chris Mandingo, Clark Kunt, Clint Torres, Cody Wellch Klondyke, Colin Grey, Corey James Caster, Coti Blayne, Crash Bandikok, Dakota Rain, Dante Diamond, Davion Summers, DeVery Bess, Devin G. Dame, Devon Ayers, Dionysus W Khaos, Diseal Tanks Roberts, D-Luv Saviyon, Dominic Demornay, Dominic Von Strap, D-Rex, Dylan Kane, E. M. Shaun, Eddie C. Broadway, Emilio, Erick LaRue, Flex Jonez, Freddy Prinze Charming, Gabe King, Gage Gatlyn,

George De Micheal, Greyson Bolt, Gunner Gatlyn, Gus Magendor, Hawk Stuart, Harry Pi, Holden Michael, Howie Feltersnatch, Hurricane Savage, J Breezy St James, Jack E. Dickinson, Jack King, Jake Van Camp, Jamel Knight, Jenson C. Dean, Johnnie Blackheart, Jonah Godfather of DRAG, Jordan Allen, Jordan Reighn, Joshua K. Mann, Joshua Micheals, Juan Kerr, Julius M. SeizeHer, Jude Lawless, Justin Cider, Justin Luvan, Justin Sider, K'ne Cole, Kameo Dupree, Kenneth J. Squires, King Dante, King Ramsey, Jack Inman, Kody Sky, Koomah, Kristian Kyler, Kruz Mhee, Linda Hermann-Chasin, Luke Ateraz, Lyle Love-It, Macximus, Marcus Mayhem, Marty Brown, Master Cameron Eric Leon, Max Hardswell, MaXx Decco, Michael Christian, Mike Oxready, Miles Long, Mr-Charlie Smith, Nanette D'angelo Sylvan, Nolan Neptune, Orion Blaze Browne, Owlejandro Monroe, Papa Cherry, Papi Chulo, Papi Chulo Doll, Persian Prince, Phantom, Pierce Gabriel, Rasta Boi Punany, Rico M Taylor, Rock McGroyn, Rocky Valentino, Rogue DRAG King, Romeo Sanchez, Rychard "Alpha" Le'Sabre, Ryder Knightly, Ryder Long, Sam Masterson, Sammy Silver, Santana Romero, Scorpio, Shane Rebel Caine, Shook ByNature, Silk Steele Prince, SirMandingo Thatis, Smitty O'Toole, Soco Dupree, Spacee Kadett, Starr Masters, Stefan LeDude, Stefon Royce Iman, Stefon SanDiego, Stormm, Teddy Michael, Thug Passion, Travis Luvermore, Travis Hard, Trey C. Michaels, Trigger Montgomery, Tyler Manhattan, Viciouse Slick, Vinnie Marconi, Welland Dowd, William Vanity Matrix, Wulf Von Monroe, Xander Havoc, and Xavier Bottoms.

Book 5:   DRAG411's
"DRAG Stories"

Funny stories shared with Todd Kachinski Kottmeier including the following contributors of DRAG Stories to include Chance Wise, Anson Reign, Tiffani Middlesexx, Rico Taylor, Todd Kachinski Kottmeier, Bob Taylor, Stefon Royce Iman, Candi Samples, Alexis Mateo, Naomi Wynters, Dmentia Divinyl, Bruce Lacie, Kennedy Wendy, Chastity Rose, Miss GiGi, Angel gLamar, Patricia Grand, Shook ByNature, Lady Guy, Eunyce Raye, Charley Marie Coutora, Jezzie Bell, Lamar Kellam, Jayden St. James, Rachelle Ann Summers, Champagne T Bordeaux, Gilda Golden, Daisha Monet, Vivika D'Angelo, Rachel Boheme, Esme Rodriguez, and MaNu Da Original.

Book 6:   DRAG411's
"DRAG Mother, DRAG Father" Honoring Mentors

Performers look to DRAG mothers, DRAG fathers, friends, and fans for insight, compassion, and guidance as mentors. This book honors those special people. Over 140 entertainers contributed wisdom and words for this historical book, making it the largest project of its nature in GLBTQ history and the first published book on male and female mentors.

Commentary shared with Todd Kachinski Kottmeier included the following contributors of DRAG Parents to includee AJ Menendez, Vinnie Marconi, Mis Sadistic, Todd Kachinski Kottmeier, Bob Taylor, Taina Norell, Andrew Stratton, Horchata Horchata, David Warner, Gianna Love, Trinity Taylor, Domunique Jazmin Vizcaya, Brittany Moore, PurrZsa Kyttyn, Jake Lickus, Shelita Taylor, Adriana Manchez, MiMi Welch, China Taylor, Armondis Bone't, Monique Trudeau, Simeon Codfish, Diamond Dupree, Stefon Royce Iman, Jayden Stjames, Demonica da Bomb, Colin Grey, Christopher Todd Guy, Celyndra Lashay Clyne, Candice St. James, Justin Barnes Williams, Ivanna Dooche, London Taylor Douglas, Christina Alexandria Victoria Regina Lowe, Bianca DeMonet, Critiqa Mann, Jazmen Andrews, AJ Allen, TotiYanah Diamond, D' Marco Knight, Chip Matthews, Mirage Montrese, India Starr Simms, Jade S Stratton, Emerald Divine, Elysse Giovanni, Vanity Halston, Kristofer Reynolds, Akasha Uravitch, Adriana Fuentes, Erykah Mirage, Felicity Ferraro, Joey Payge, Rhiannon Todd, Vicious Slick, Amirage Saling, Tori Sass, Chy'enne Valentino, and Robbi Lynn.

Book 7:   DRAG411's
"Spotlight Today"

It was the World's Largest Paperback Magazine for Impersonators and Fans when it premiered with over 175 pages. DRAG411 no longer prints Spotlight Today Magazine, but here is the re-release of the groundbreaking first edition. Complete articles by Vinnie Marconi, Denise Russell, Tiffani T. Middlesexx, Kristofer Reynolds, Magenta Alexandria Dupree, Butch Daddy, Vivikah Kayson-Raye, Makanoe, Amanda Lay, Thomas DeVoyd, Kevin B. Reed, Glenn Storm, and over 150 impersonators from around the world.

Book 8:   DRAG411's
"DRAG Queen Guide"

Almost two hundred female impersonators around the world share over a thousand insightful comments in forty-one chapters.

Commentary shared with Todd Kachinski Kottmeier included the following contributors of Official DRAG Queen and Female Impersonator Handbook to include Alana Summers, Alexis Marie Von Furstenburg, Alize', Aloe Vera, Alysin Wonderland, Amanda Bone DeMornay, Amanda Lay, Amanda Roberts, Amy DeMilo, Anastasia Fallon, Angie Ovahness, Anita Mandinite, Appolonia Cruz, Ashlyn Tyler, Aurora Tr'Nele Michelle, Azia Sparks, Barbie Dayne, Barbra Herr, Beverly LaSalle, Bianca DeMonet, Bianca Lynn Breeze, Blair Michaels, Boxxa Vine, Brittany T Moore, Britney Towers, Brandi Amara Skyy, Brooke Lynn Bradshaw, Candi Samples, Candi Stratton, Candy Sugar, Cathy Craig, Catia Lee Love, CeCe Georgia, Cee-Cee LaRouge-Avalon, Celeste Starr, Chad Michaels, Chevon Davis, Cheyenne Desoto Mykels, Chi Chi Lalique, Christina Collins, Chrystal Conners, Claudia B Eautiful, Coca Mesa, Coco St James, Damiana LaRoux, Dana Scrumptious, Danyel Vasquez, Dee Gregory, Delores T. Van-Cartier, Demonica DaBaum, Denise Russell, Diamond Dunhill, Diva Lilo, Diva Savage, Dove, EdriAna Treviño, Elle Emenopé, Elysse Giovanni, Erica James, Esmé Rodríguez, Estella Sweet, Eunyce Raye, Eva Nichole Distruction, Faleasha Savage, Felicia Minor, Felicity Frockaccino, Gigi Masters, Ginger Alley, Ginger Gigi Diamond, Ginger Kaye Belmont, Glitz Glam, Grecia Montes D' Occa, Heather Daniels, Hennessy Heart, Hershae Chocolatae, Holy McGrail, Hope B Childs, Horchata, India Brooks, India Ferrah, Ivy Profen, Izzy Adahl, Jaclyn St James, Jade Iroq, Jade Sotomayor, Jade Taylor Stratton, Jamie-Ree Swan, Jennifer Warner, Jessica Brooks, Jexa Ren'ae Van de Kamp, Joey Brooks, Jonny Pride, Kamelle Toe, Karma Jayde Addams, Kelly Turner, Mama Savannah Georgia, Mr. Kenneth Blake, Kamden T. Rage, Kira Stone-St James, Kirby Kolby, Kita Rose, Krysta Radiance, Lacie Bruce, Lady Jasmine Michaels, Lady Pearl, Lady Sabrina, Latrice Royale, LaTonga Manchez, Leona Barr, Lexi Alexander, Lilo Monroe, Lindsay Carlton, Lucinda Holliday, Lunara Sky, Lupita Chiquita Michaels Alexander, Madam Diva Divine, Mahog Anny, Makayla Michelle Davis Diamond, Mariah Cherry, Maxine Padlock, Melody Mayheim, Menaje E'toi, Mercede Andrews, Mi$hal, Mia Fierce, Michelle Leigh Sterling, Miss Diva Savage, Miss GiGi, Misty Eyez, Mitze Peterbilt, Monica Mystique, Montrese Lamar Hollar, Morgana DeRaven, Muffy Vanbeaverhousen, Natasha Richards, Nathan Loveland, Nicole Paige Brooks, Nikki

Garcia, Nostalgia Todd Ronin, Olivia St James, Paige Sinclair, Pandora DeCeption, Pheobe James, Reia'Cheille Lucious, Robyn Demornay, Robyn Graves, Rhonda Sheer, Rose Murphy, Ruby Diamond NY, Ruby Holiday, Ryan Royale, Rychard "Alpha" Le'Sabre, Rye Seronie, Sable Monay, Sabrina Kayson-Raye, Samantha St Clair, Sanaa Raelynn, Sapphire T. Mylan, Sasha Phillips, Savannah Rivers, Savannah Stevens, Selina Kyle, Sha'day Halston-St James, ShaeShae LaReese, Shamya Banx, Shana Nicole, Shaunna Rai, Sierra Foxx White, Sierra Santana, Sonja Jae Savage, Stella D'oro, Strawberry Whip, Sugarpill, Tasha Carter, Tanna Blake, Taquella Roze, Tawdri Hipburn, Taylor Rockland, Tempest DuJour, Tiffani T. Middlesexx, Traci Russell, Trudy Tyler, Vanessa del Rey, Velveeta WhoreMel, Vera Delmar, Vicky Summers, Vita DeVine, Vivian Sorensin, Vivian Von Brokenhymen, Vivika D'Angelo-Steele, Wendy G. Kennedy, Willmuh Dickfit, Wynter Storm, Yasmine Alexander and ZuZu Bella.

Book 9:   DRAG411's (Two Comedy Scripts)
"Best Said Dead" and **"Following Wynter"**

Best Said Dead examines in funny conversations those brief minutes after a person dies. Many religions and beliefs define different paths for each of us. Rarely do we discuss those precious moments between death and the final destination. This comedy opens the possibilities that for a moment, a person vanishes into the memories in their mind. Any part can be male, female, or ambiguous.

Following Wynter is a hilarious comedy play. Ethan discovers his newlywed husband is the flamboyant DRAG queen Wynter Storm in this whimsical farce with an important message of believing in yourself and your friends. . . even if your friend is Serena Silver. Any part can be male, female, or ambiguous.

Book 10:   DRAG411's
"DRAG World"
The contributing writers of DRAG411's "Spotlight Magazine," the World's Largest Paperback Magazine for Impersonators and Fans when it premiered in 2012 with over 175 pages, created this companion book. DRAG411 no longer prints Spotlight Today Magazine, but above you will find Book 7 is the re-release of the groundbreaking first edition. Complete chapters on DRAG Marketing by DRAG411.
Complimentary articles on Confidence, Duct Tape, Music Selection, Living Divinely, authentic stage presence, Pageants, having fun performing, jewelry, legislative information from the United States and around the world, the Old School performers, Virgin stage performers, and payday from contributing writers including Denise Russell, Jay Santana, Chance Wise, Vivikah Kayson-Raye, AJ Menedez, Glenn Storm, Freddy

Prinze Charming, Gage Gatlyn, Kevin B. Reed, and over 100 impersonators from around the world!

Other books from the Best Selling author
The Infamous Todd Kachinski Kottmeier

"Turn Around Bright Eyes, The DRAG Queen Killer"

Few crimes in gay history rocked a nation as great as The DRAG Queen Killer. The country seemed paralyzed from the first ring of the chain tapping on the concrete, as they pulled Cassandra to her death, until the very last brutal killing. The murderous rampage seemed buried amongst the media suffering from a barrage of tales from the 9-11 terrorist attacks.

"CommUnity of Transition"

We sent over a thousand invitations to the transgender community around the world asking them to share wisdom, advice, and compassion for those questioning or struggling. No restraints, using topics they created, as they guided the conversation over forty chapters and fifty topics. By the close, these remarkable people had created the largest compilation book in transgender history. They opened their heart with these words.

NOTE: *This book is "lightly edited" to reflect the intent and form of over one hundred transgender contributors. Unedited photographs "before and after" come from actual contributing transgender writers.*

"Joey Brooks, The Show Must Go On"
By Joey Brooks and Todd Kachinski Kottmeier

Joey Brooks, The Show Must Go On is the story of The First Lady of Ybor from the days of El Goya to present day. Female Impersonator, Show director, hostess, author…
"Old school, new school, no school… who gives a shit? I'm too old to go to school. I barely remember last week. When I get too old to remember what the fuck I did when I was young …ger, I'll just open one of these books and laugh my ass off. I wonder how many other queens had this much fun becoming one of the icons of their community. Too funny. I just called myself an icon. Hell, I must be a queen. Only a female impersonator could call themselves a diva, a queen, a star without people giggling behind her back. Giggling is good. A twenty-dollar bill is better."

"Two Days Past Dead"

The Author's First Published Book

It is hard to be the good guy when you succeed so well being bad. This is the Auggie Summer's dilemma his entire life. The story, based loosely on the tales of The Infamous Todd, follows the precocious child. His story begins with selling candy in 9th grade where he catches not only the attention of the press but also amusement of the drug cartel early in its' own infancy. Auggie Summers finds himself in the forefront of one of the most dangerous organizations on Earth.

"Waiting On God"
The Author's Humorist Novel

Learn to live after the doctors tell you "that are dying." A humorist essay on embracing funny moments and to create an environment around you that makes people not only laugh, but also be inspired by your strength.